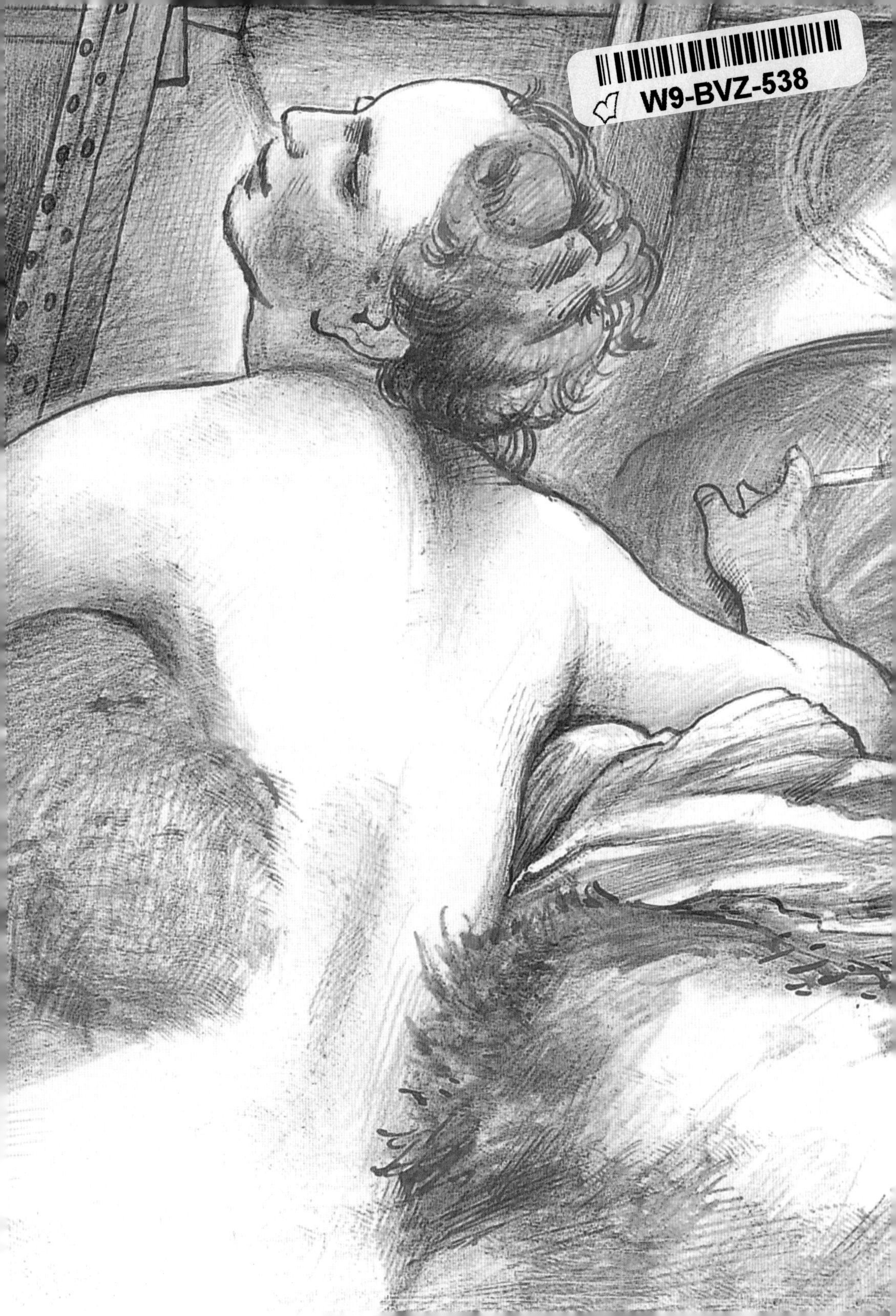

INTRODUCTION BY SETH

It is remarkable that an artist could be such an innovator, so ahead of the crowd and could have produced such an impressive list of comics novels and yet still somehow be overlooked when people talk about "the graphic novel." However, this is the case with Raymond Briggs. Sadly, his name doesn't come up as often as it should.

Don't get me wrong—it's not as if he is unknown or under-appreciated. Briggs is a well respected and much honoured artist, and he very well may be one of the most successful living cartoonists in the world, with over three million of his books sold. However, not many people see him as a cartoonist per se. It's simply the old story of pigeonholing. He started out as a children's book author, and the label has stuck.

Will Eisner's *A Contract With God,* published in 1978, is often trotted out as the first official graphic novel (ignoring the fact that it is actually a collection of short stories and not a "novel" at all). Why is it that no one has ever noticed that Briggs' *The Snowman,* which came out the same year, is actually a much better candidate for the title? In fact, Briggs had two full length, self contained "graphic novels" published several years earlier: *Father Christmas* and *Father Christmas Goes On Holiday.* The fact that these were written for children

shouldn't remove them from the contest. But there is the rub. Children. It's that connection with children's books that has kept him on the sidelines.

It looks to me that this book, *Gentleman Jim,* is the work that marks the dividing line in his career. Before this most of his works could be still labeled as intended primarily for children. *Gentleman Jim* is unmistakably a work aimed at an adult audience. I suppose I could imagine a child reading and enjoying it—it is a funny book—but I'd have to guess that an older reader would be needed to truly appreciate its dry tone and the pathos in poor Jim and his muddled thinking. Briggs has since gone on to produce a good half dozen comic albums for adults and yet he is still regularly left off that list of important cartoonists. Had his career begun with *Gentleman Jim,* I suspect this would not be the case.

Forgive me for going on about this—I certainly don't want to waste this introduction nitpicking which books should fit where in an imaginary history of the modern "graphic novel." I also don't wish to belabor the point and give the wrong impression that Mr. Briggs is languishing in some cartoon limbo. Certainly his lasting importance is alone assured by the critical attention he received for *When The Wind Blows.*

Published in 1982, the book is almost universally recognized as one of the most touching and powerful treatments of nuclear war. Like most readers, this was the book where I first discovered Briggs, and I was moved tremendously by it. His decision to focus on two such simple, vulnerable characters as the Bloggs, placed in a situation so far beyond their comprehension, was an inspired choice. It was a reading experience that has always remained with me. There are very few comics narratives that have brought an actual tear to my eye. Perhaps it has been the only one.

A few years later I was surprised to discover that the Bloggs had appeared in an earlier book, *Gentleman Jim*. I didn't recognize it then, but now it is obvious that the Bloggs are the Briggs, Raymond's own parents. Looking at it today, I think I can guess that his decision to use the Bloggs in *When The Wind Blows* may not have been that much of a choice after all.

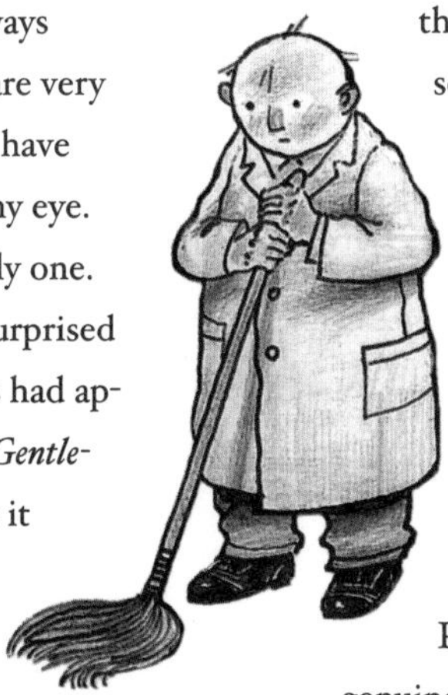

I started to understand this when I read his *Unlucky Wally* books. Something in the mother struck a familiar chord in my mind. This was entirely confirmed in 1998 when he published his wonderful memoir of his parents, *Ethel & Ernest*. Though less broadly caricatured in manner, it is unmistakable that Ethel and Ernest are Jim and Hilda Bloggs. The death of the mother in *Unlucky Wally* mirrors Briggs' own mother's death, as portrayed in *Ethel & Ernest*. Looking back over his body of work you start to see Briggs' parents everywhere in his books. I might hazard a guess that Raymond Briggs' complex relationship with his mother and father is the primary, seminal force in his drive as an artist. It's a rich vein and each time he has returned to these figures they have grown deeper. And he does seem compelled to return to them again and again.

I have to say, too, they are quite unique creations these Jim and Hilda types. So sweet and yet so foolish. You laugh at them but you also pity them. And admire them somehow, too. They are forthright and honest and earthy. Perpetual children, in a manner. A genuinely sad quality is transmitted about them as well. They draw out a deep empathy from us. Jim and Hilda remind me in many ways of my own parents, and perhaps that is why they appeal to me so greatly.

I'm glad to see this edition of *Gentleman Jim* back in print. It is an utterly charming book. I would like to see all of his books back in print. Raymond Briggs is a great cartoonist. I hold him in the highest regard. A marvelous craftsman, a hard worker and a thoughtful, original and sensitive artist.

Drawn & Quarterly
Post Office Box 48056
Montreal, Quebec
Canada H2V 4S8
www.drawnandquarterly.com

First Drawn & Quarterly edition: June 2008.
Printed in Hong Kong.
10 9 8 7 6 5 4 3 2 1

Library and Archives Canada Cataloguing in Publication
Briggs, Raymond
        Gentleman Jim / Raymond Briggs.
ISBN 978-1-897299-36-4
        1. Graphic novels. 11. Title.
PN6737.B7G46 2007   741.5'941   C2007-904717-3

Distributed in the USA by:
Farrar, Straus and Giroux
18 West 18th Street
New York, NY 10011
Orders: 888.330.8477

Distributed in Canada by:
Raincoast Books
9050 Shaughnessy Street
Vancouver, BC V6P 6E5
Orders: 800.663.5714

GENTLEMAN JIM

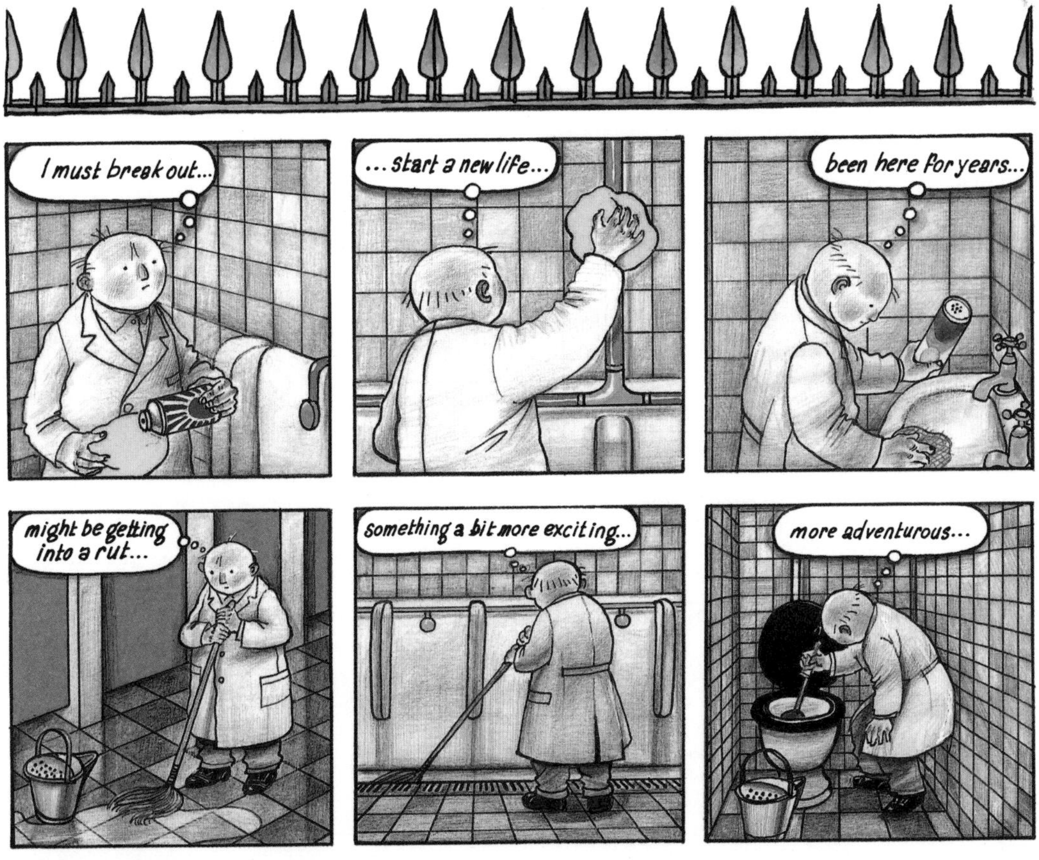

I must break out...
... start a new life...
been here for years...
might be getting into a rut...
something a bit more exciting...
more adventurous...
.. something with more of a challenge...
There's not much opportunity for self-advancement in toilets...

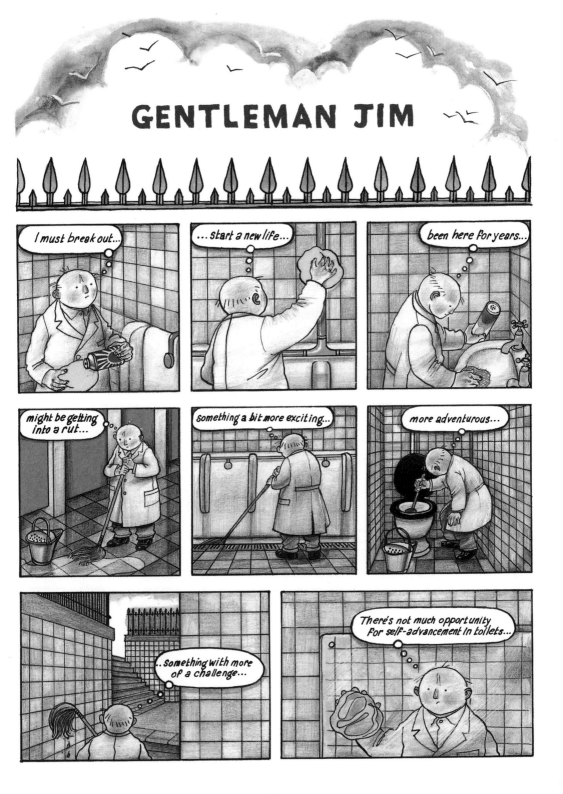

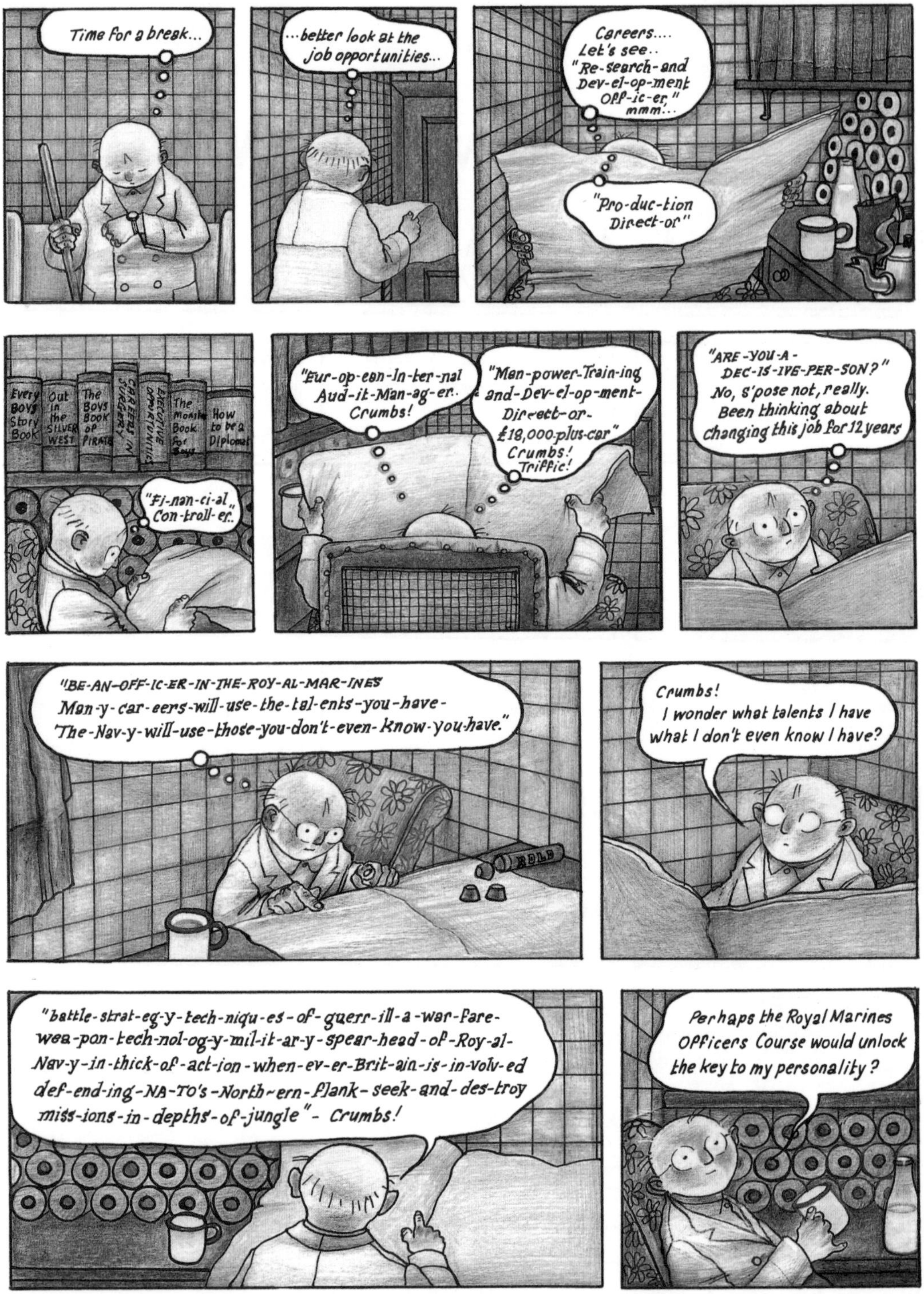
Time for a break...
...better look at the job opportunities...
Careers.... Let's see.. "Re-search-and Dev-el-op-ment Off-ic-er," mmm...
"Pro-duc-tion Direct-or"
Every Boys Story Book
Out in the Silver West
The Boys Book of Pirate
Careers in Surgery
Executive Opportunities
How to be a Diplomat
"Fi-nan-ci-al Con-troll-er."
"Eur-op-ean-In-ter-nal Aud-it-Man-ag-er. Crumbs!
"Man-power-Train-ing and-Dev-el-op-ment-Direct-or-£18,000-plus-car" Crumbs! Triffic!
"ARE-YOU-A-DEC-IS-IVE-PER-SON?" No, s'pose not, really. Been thinking about changing this job for 12 years
"BE-AN-OFF-IC-ER-IN-THE-ROY-AL-MAR-INES Man-y-car-eers-will-use-the-tal-ents-you-have-'The-Nav-y-will-use-those-you-don't-even-know-you-have."
Crumbs! I wonder what talents I have what I don't even know I have?
"battle-strat-eg-y-tech-niqu-es-of-guerr-ill-a-war-fare-wea-pon-tech-nol-og-y-mil-it-ar-y-spear-head-of-Roy-al-Nav-y-in-thick-of-act-ion-when-ev-er-Brit-ain-is-in-volv-ed def-end-ing-NA-TO's-North-ern-flank-seek-and-des-troy miss-ions-in-depths-of-jungle" - Crumbs!
Perhaps the Royal Marines Officers Course would unlock the key to my personality?

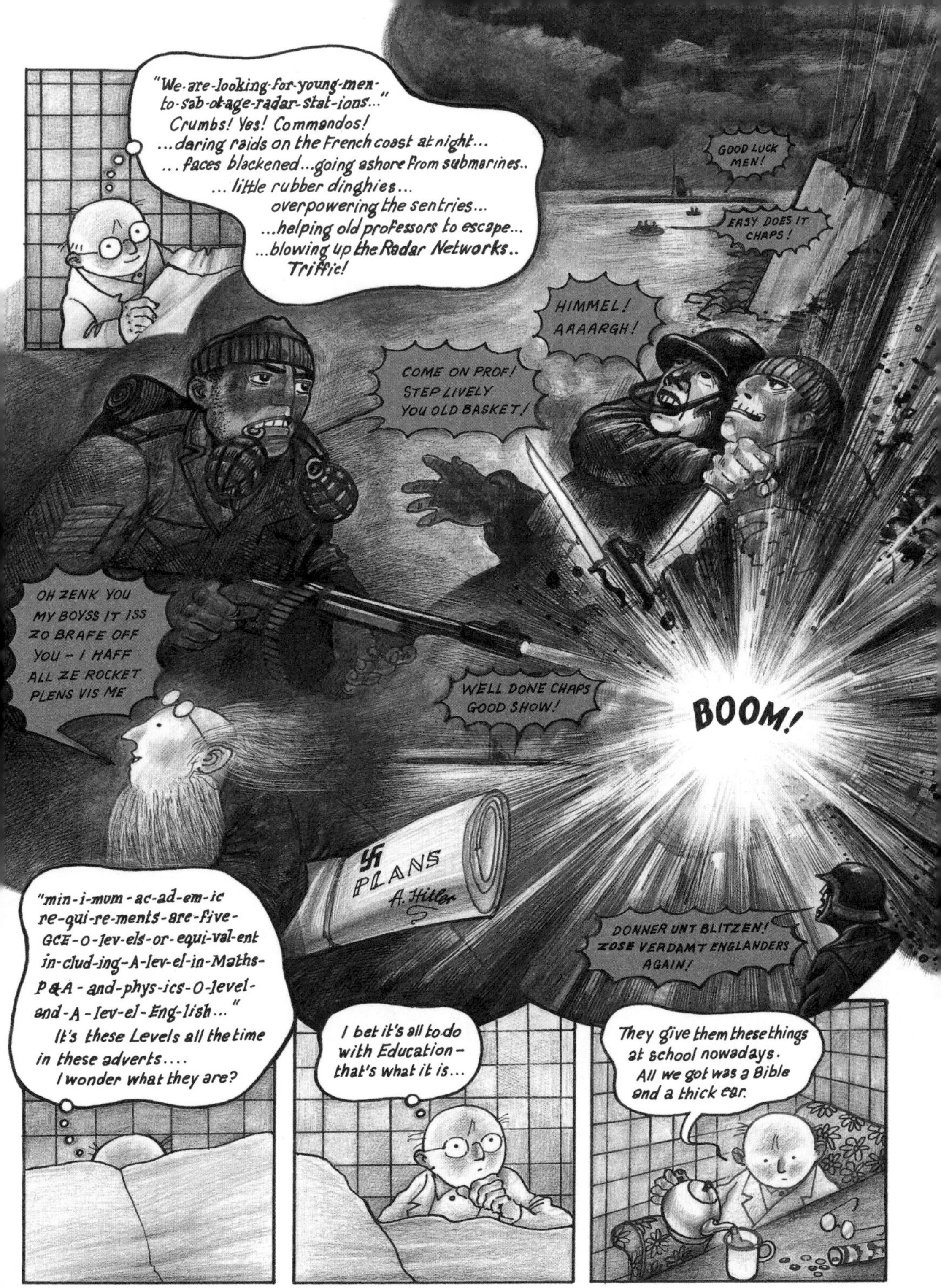
"We-are-looking-for-young-men-to-sab-ot-age-radar-stat-ions..." Crumbs! Yes! Commandos! ...daring raids on the French coast at night... ...faces blackened...going ashore from submarines.. ...little rubber dinghies... overpowering the sentries... ...helping old professors to escape... ...blowing up the Radar Networks.. Triffic!
GOOD LUCK MEN!
EASY DOES IT CHAPS!
HIMMEL! AAAARGH!
COME ON PROF! STEP LIVELY YOU OLD BASKET!
OH ZENK YOU MY BOYSS IT ISS ZO BRAFE OFF YOU - I HAFF ALL ZE ROCKET PLENS VIS ME
WELL DONE CHAPS GOOD SHOW!
BOOM!
PLANS
A. Hitler
DONNER UNT BLITZEN! ZOSE VERDAMT ENGLANDERS AGAIN!
"min-i-mum-ac-ad-em-ic re-qui-re-ments-are-five-GCE-O-lev-els-or-equi-val-ent in-clud-ing-A-lev-el-in-Maths-P&A-and-phys-ics-O-level-and-A-lev-el-Eng-lish..." It's these Levels all the time in these adverts.... I wonder what they are?
I bet it's all to do with Education - that's what it is...
They give them these things at school nowadays. All we got was a Bible and a thick ear.

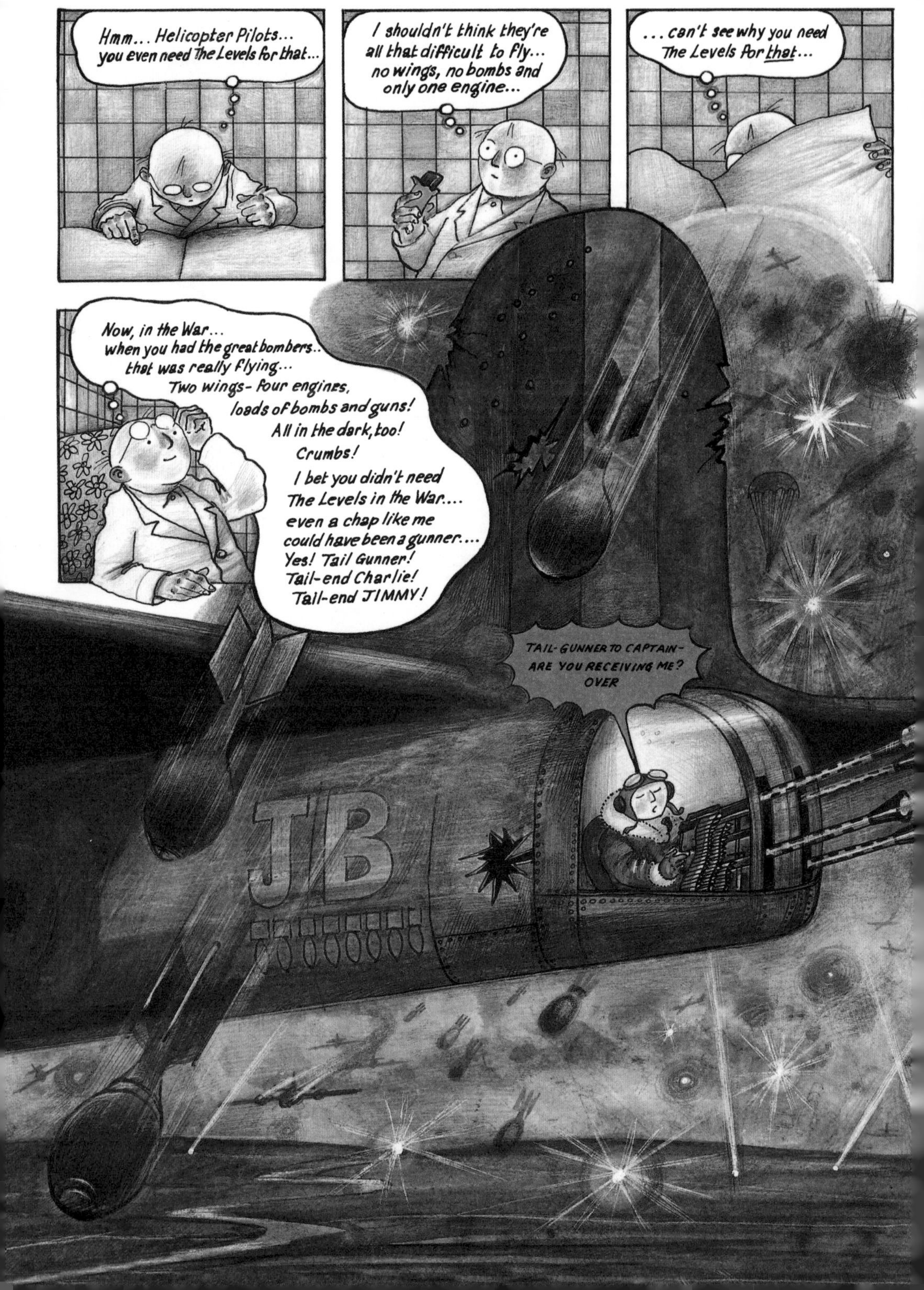
Hmm... Helicopter Pilots... you even need The Levels for that...
I shouldn't think they're all that difficult to fly... no wings, no bombs and only one engine...
...can't see why you need The Levels for that...
Now, in the War... when you had the great bombers.. that was really flying... Two wings- four engines, loads of bombs and guns! All in the dark, too! Crumbs! I bet you didn't need The Levels in the War.... even a chap like me could have been a gunner.... Yes! Tail Gunner! Tail-end Charlie! Tail-end JIMMY!
TAIL-GUNNER TO CAPTAIN- ARE YOU RECEIVING ME? OVER
JB

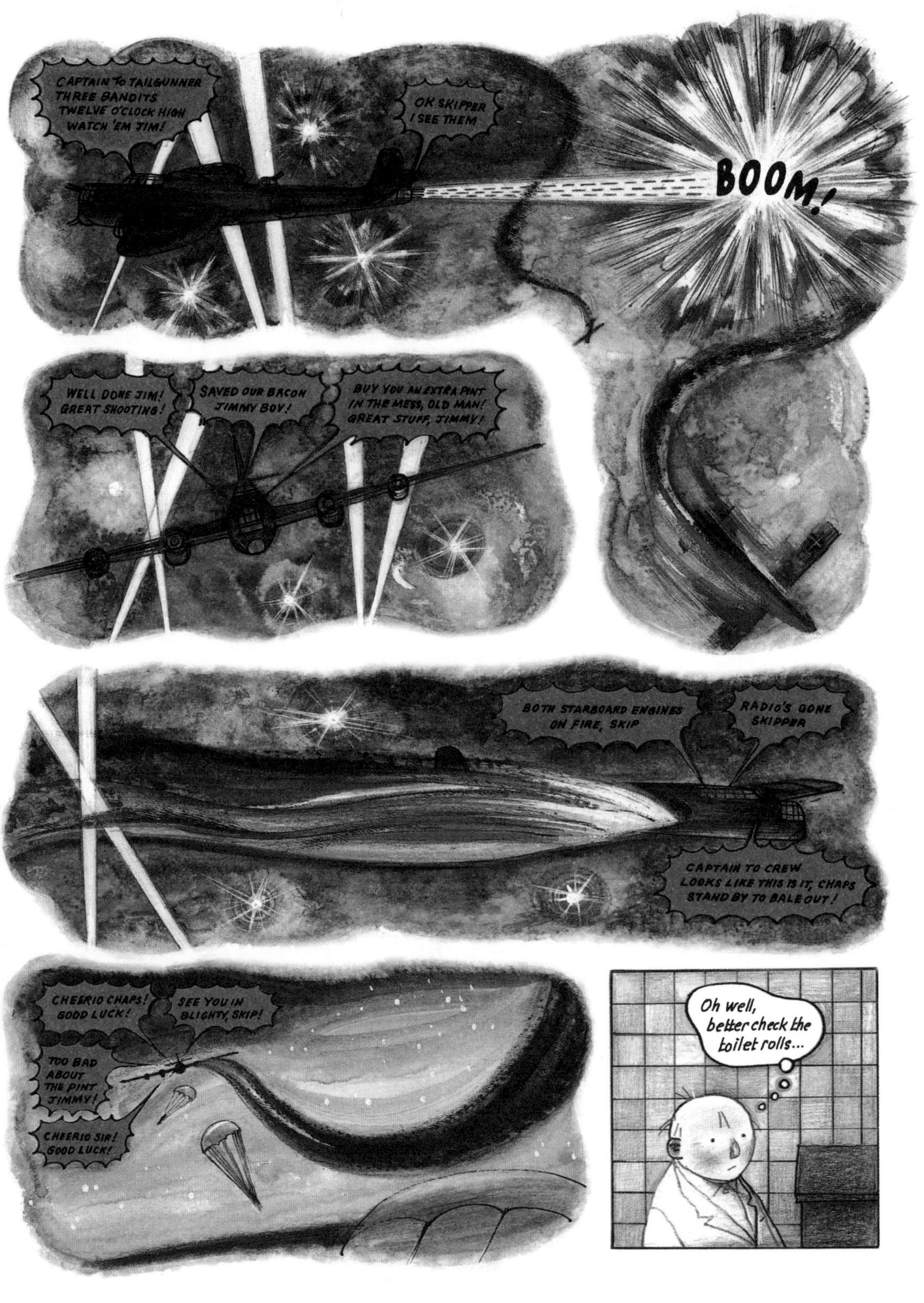
CAPTAIN TO TAILGUNNER THREE BANDITS TWELVE O'CLOCK HIGH WATCH 'EM JIM!
OK SKIPPER I SEE THEM
BOOM!
WELL DONE JIM! GREAT SHOOTING!
SAVED OUR BACON JIMMY BOY!
BUY YOU AN EXTRA PINT IN THE MESS, OLD MAN! GREAT STUFF, JIMMY!
BOTH STARBOARD ENGINES ON FIRE, SKIP
RADIO'S GONE SKIPPER
CAPTAIN TO CREW LOOKS LIKE THIS IS IT, CHAPS STAND BY TO BALE OUT!
CHEERIO CHAPS! GOOD LUCK!
SEE YOU IN BLIGHTY, SKIP!
TOO BAD ABOUT THE PINT JIMMY!
CHEERIO SIR! GOOD LUCK!
Oh well, better check the toilet rolls...

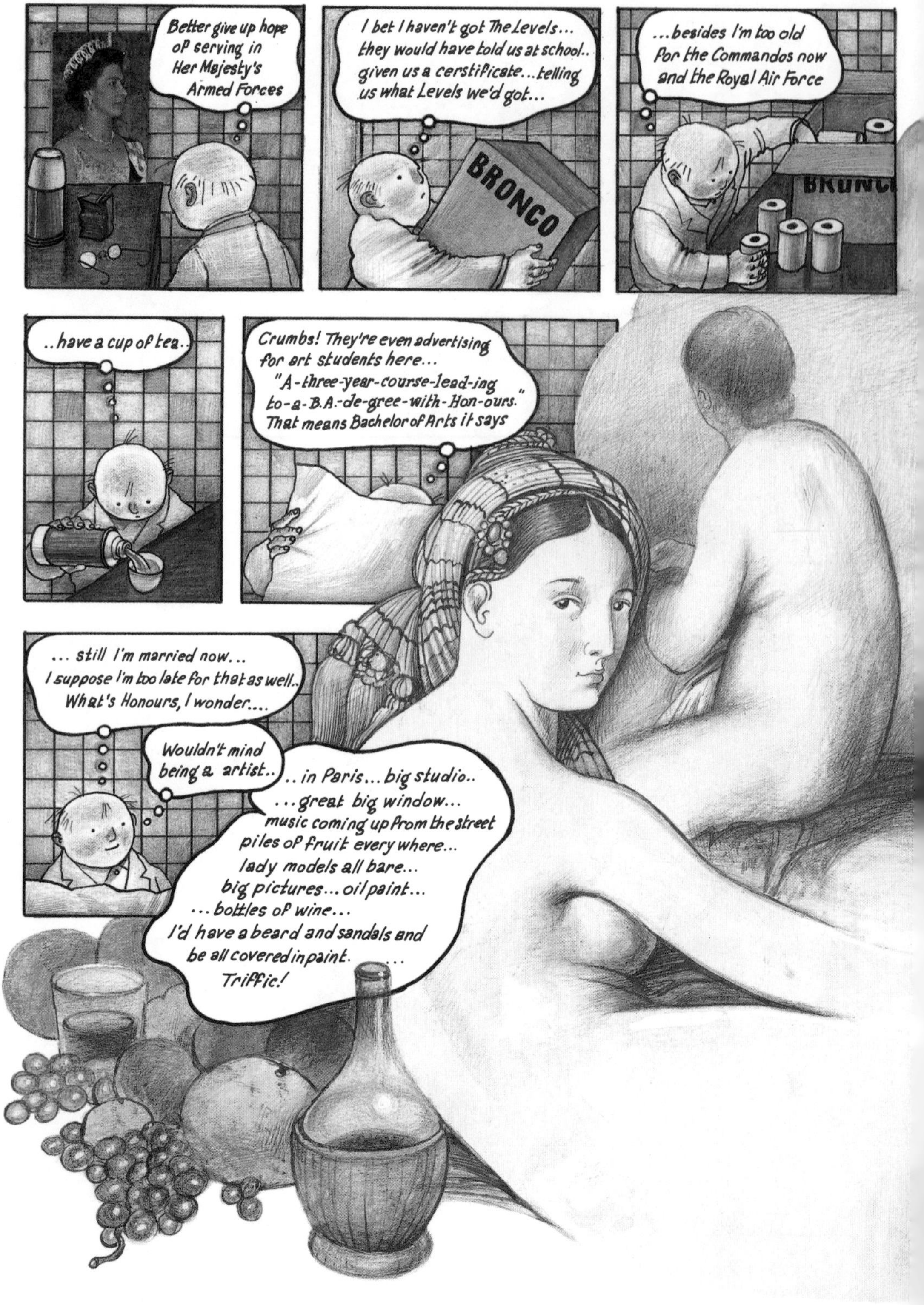
Better give up hope of serving in Her Majesty's Armed Forces
I bet I haven't got The Levels... they would have told us at school.. given us a cerstificate...telling us what Levels we'd got...
BRONCO
...besides I'm too old for the Commandos now and the Royal Air Force
BRONCO
..have a cup of tea..
Crumbs! They're even advertising for art students here... "A-three-year-course-lead-ing to-a-B.A.-de-gree-with-Hon-ours." That means Bachelor of Arts it says
... still I'm married now... I suppose I'm too late for that as well.. What's Honours, I wonder....
Wouldn't mind being a artist..
.. in Paris... big studio.. ...great big window... music coming up from the street piles of fruit every where... lady models all bare... big pictures... oil paint... ...bottles of wine... I'd have a beard and sandals and be all covered in paint. ... Triffic!

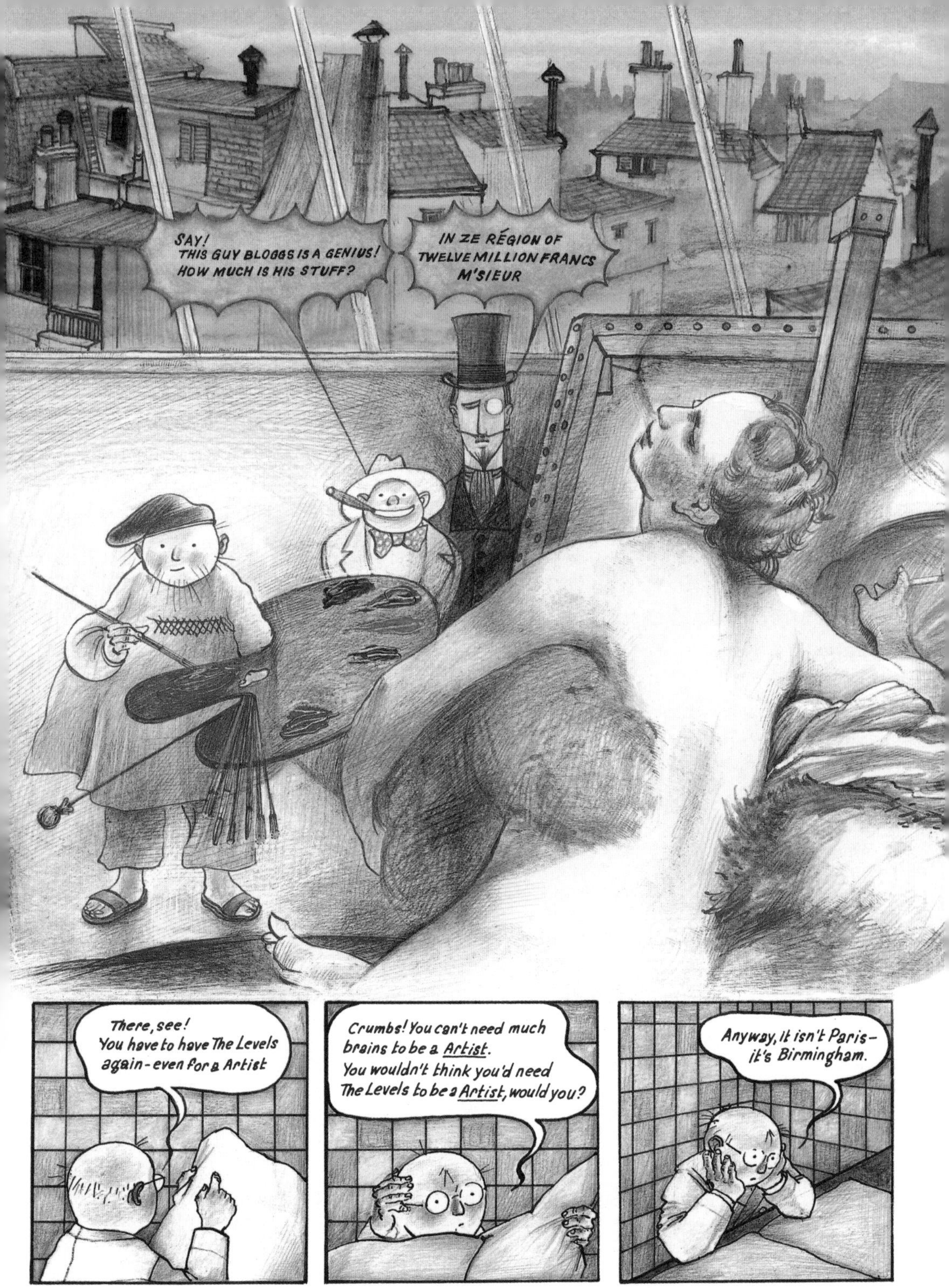
SAY!
THIS GUY BLOGGS IS A GENIUS!
HOW MUCH IS HIS STUFF?
IN ZE RÉGION OF
TWELVE MILLION FRANCS
M'SIEUR
There, see!
You have to have The Levels
again - even for a Artist
Crumbs! You can't need much
brains to be a Artist.
You wouldn't think you'd need
The Levels to be a Artist, would you?
Anyway, it isn't Paris -
it's Birmingham.

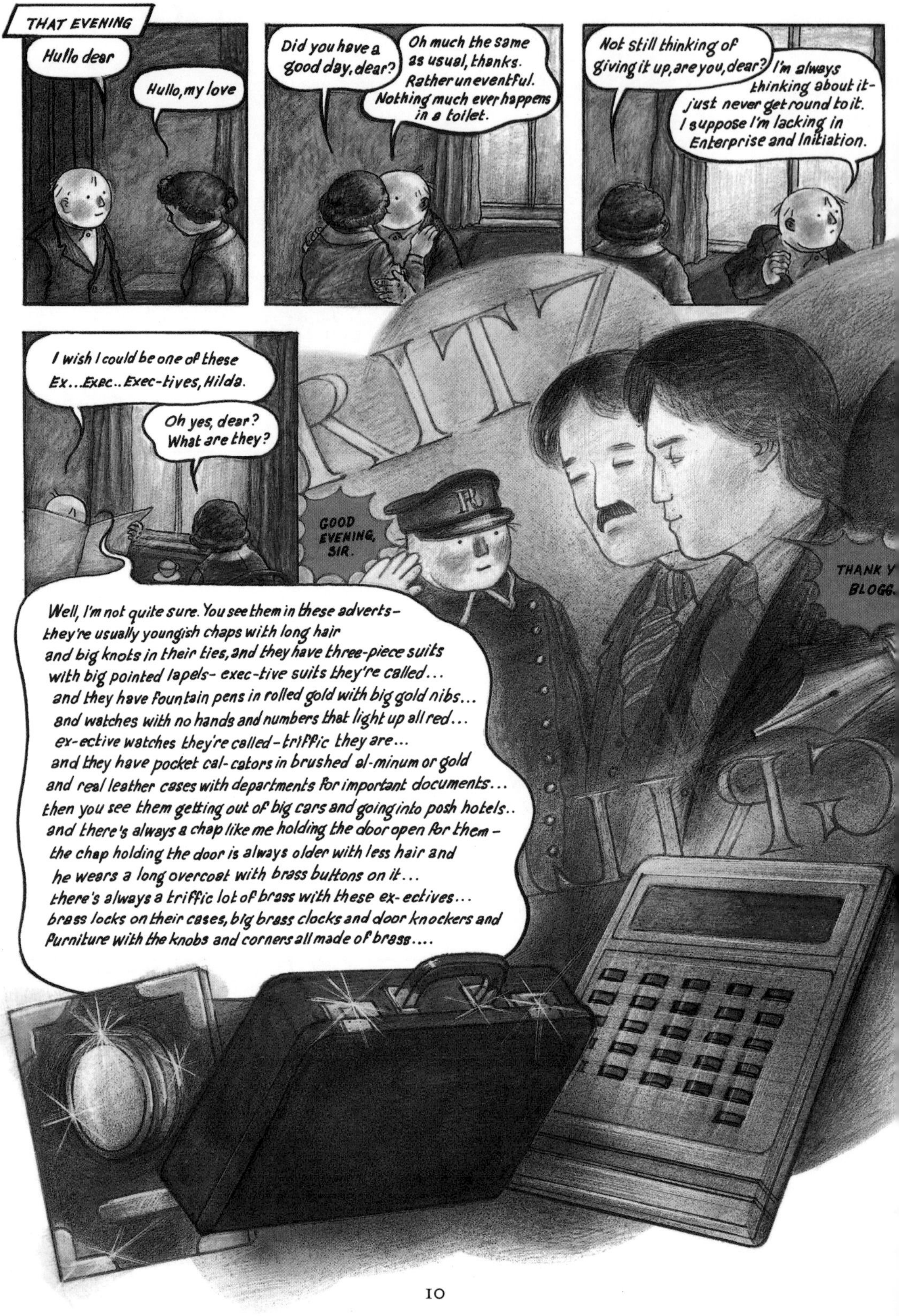
THAT EVENING
Hullo dear
Hullo, my love
Did you have a good day, dear?
Oh much the same as usual, thanks. Rather uneventful. Nothing much ever happens in a toilet.
Not still thinking of giving it up, are you, dear?
I'm always thinking about it- just never get round to it. I suppose I'm lacking in Enterprise and Initiation.
I wish I could be one of these Ex...Exec..Exec-tives, Hilda.
Oh yes, dear? What are they?
GOOD EVENING, SIR.
THANK Y
BLOGG.
Well, I'm not quite sure. You see them in these adverts- they're usually youngish chaps with long hair and big knots in their ties, and they have three-piece suits with big pointed lapels- exec-tive suits they're called... and they have fountain pens in rolled gold with big gold nibs... and watches with no hands and numbers that light up all red... ex-ective watches they're called - triffic they are... and they have pocket cal-cators in brushed al-minum or gold and real leather cases with departments for important documents... then you see them getting out of big cars and going into posh hotels.. and there's always a chap like me holding the door open for them - the chap holding the door is always older with less hair and he wears a long overcoat with brass buttons on it... there's always a triffic lot of brass with these ex-ectives... brass locks on their cases, big brass clocks and door knockers and furniture with the knobs and corners all made of brass....

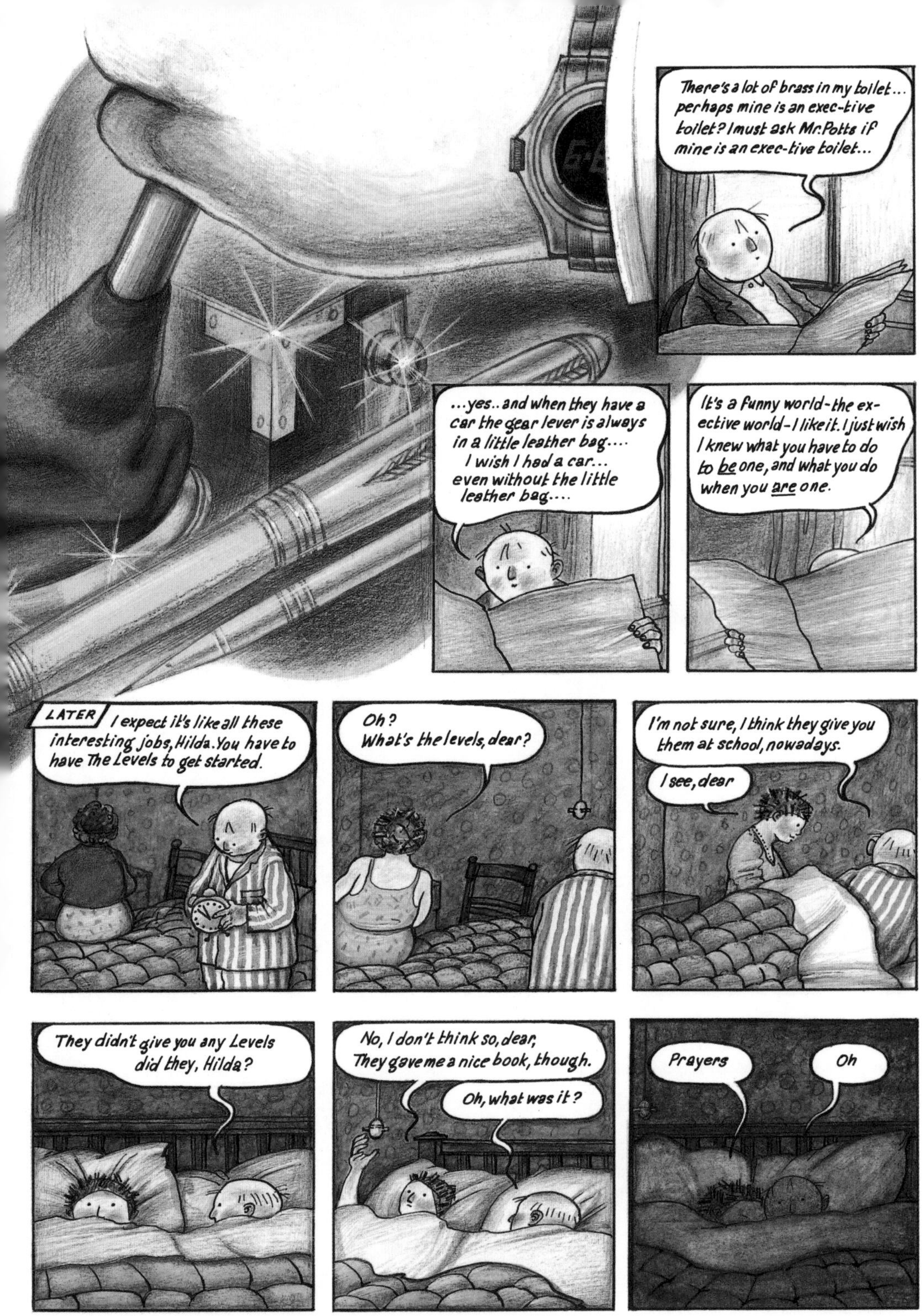

There's a lot of brass in my toilet... perhaps mine is an exec-tive toilet? I must ask Mr. Potts if mine is an exec-tive toilet...
...yes.. and when they have a car the gear lever is always in a little leather bag.... I wish I had a car... even without the little leather bag....
It's a funny world - the exective world - I like it. I just wish I knew what you have to do to be one, and what you do when you are one.
LATER
I expect it's like all these interesting jobs, Hilda. You have to have The Levels to get started.
Oh? What's the levels, dear?
I'm not sure, I think they give you them at school, nowadays.
I see, dear
They didn't give you any Levels did they, Hilda?
No, I don't think so, dear, They gave me a nice book, though.
Oh, what was it?
Prayers
Oh

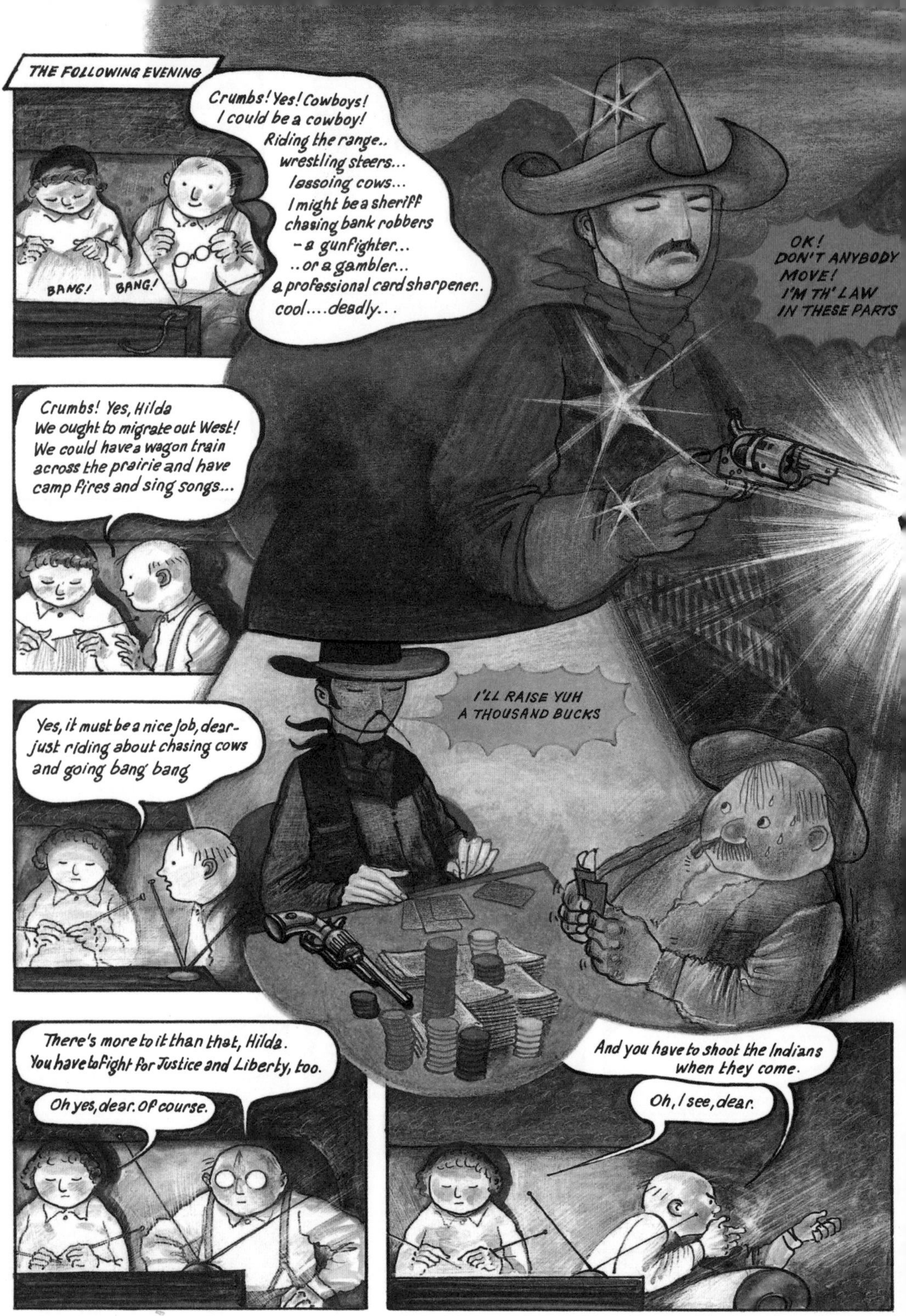
THE FOLLOWING EVENING
BANG! BANG!
Crumbs! Yes! Cowboys! I could be a cowboy! Riding the range.. wrestling steers... lassoing cows... I might be a sheriff chasing bank robbers – a gunfighter... ..or a gambler... a professional card sharpener.. cool....deadly...
OK! DON'T ANYBODY MOVE! I'M TH' LAW IN THESE PARTS
Crumbs! Yes, Hilda We ought to migrate out West! We could have a wagon train across the prairie and have camp fires and sing songs...
I'LL RAISE YUH A THOUSAND BUCKS
Yes, it must be a nice job, dear- just riding about chasing cows and going bang bang
There's more to it than that, Hilda. You have to fight for Justice and Liberty, too.
Oh yes, dear. Of course.
And you have to shoot the Indians when they come.
Oh, I see, dear.

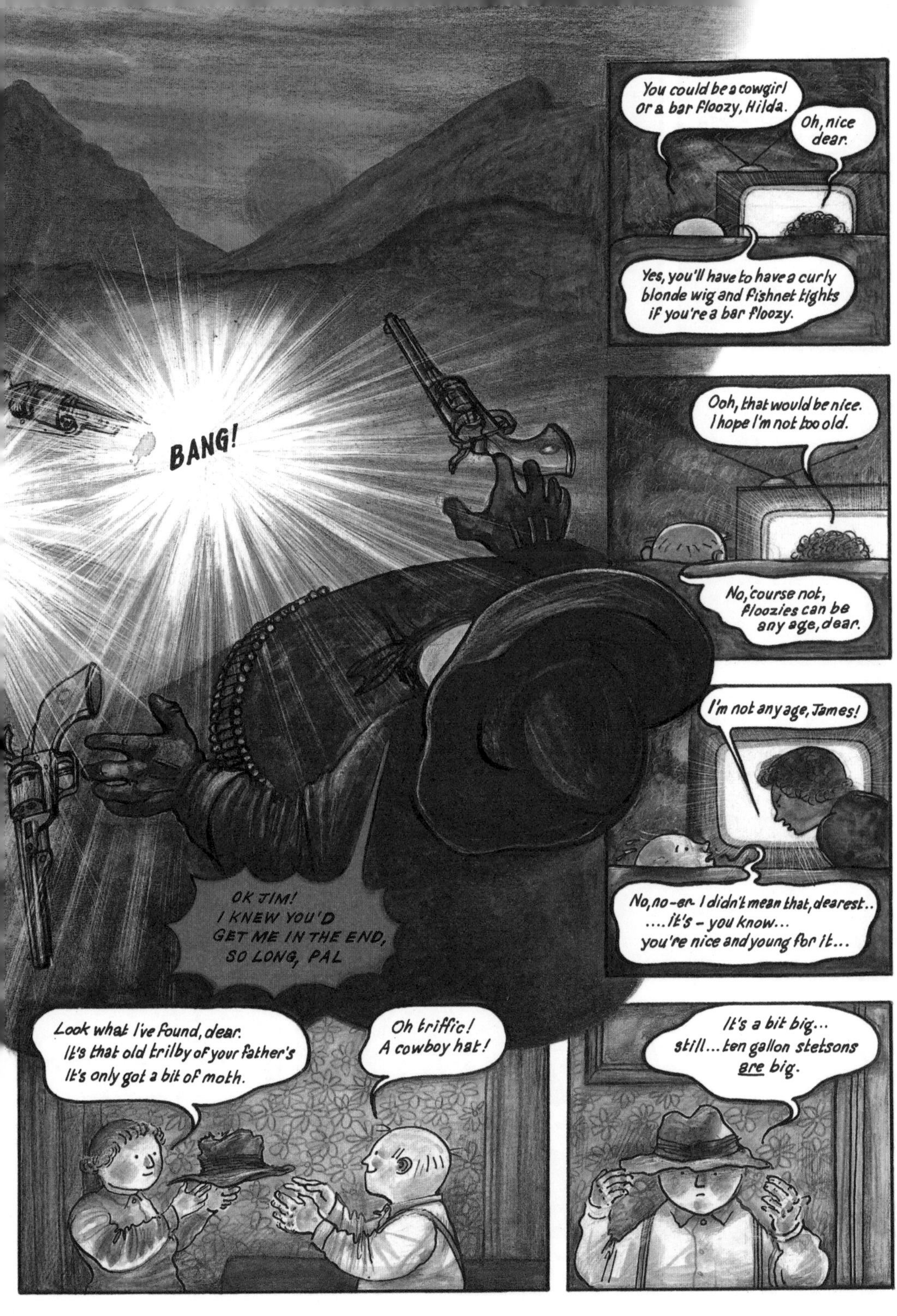
BANG!
OK JIM! I KNEW YOU'D GET ME IN THE END, SO LONG, PAL
You could be a cowgirl or a bar floozy, Hilda.
Oh, nice dear.
Yes, you'll have to have a curly blonde wig and fishnet tights if you're a bar floozy.
Ooh, that would be nice. I hope I'm not too old.
No, 'course not, floozies can be any age, dear.
I'm not any age, James!
No, no-er I didn't mean that, dearest.. ....it's - you know... you're nice and young for it...
Look what I've found, dear. It's that old trilby of your father's It's only got a bit of moth.
Oh triffic! A cowboy hat!
It's a bit big... still... ten gallon stetsons are big.

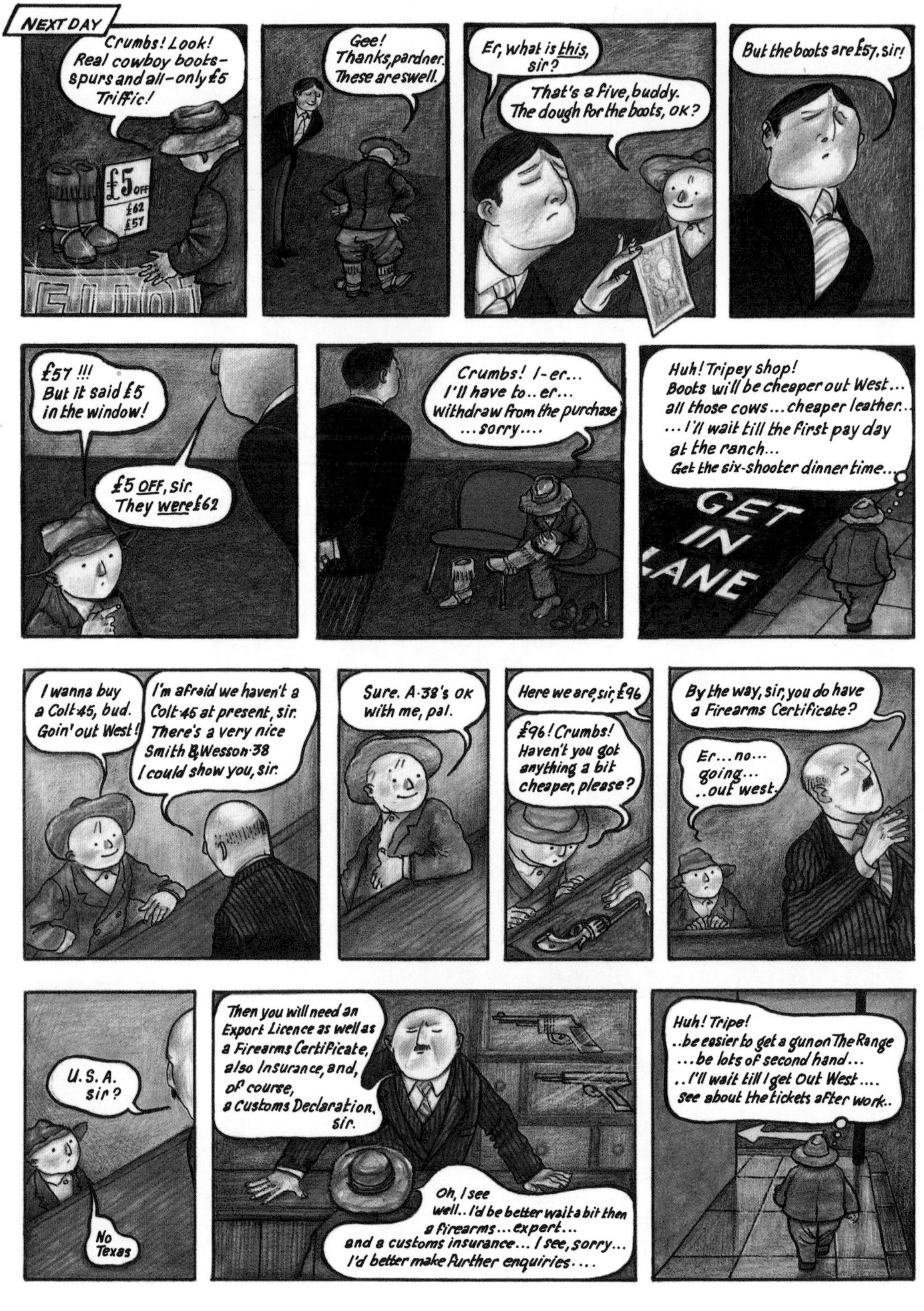
NEXT DAY
Crumbs! Look! Real cowboy boots-spurs and all-only £5 Triffic!
£5 OFF £62 £57
Gee! Thanks, pardner. These are swell.
Er, what is this, sir?
That's a five, buddy. The dough for the boots, OK?
But the boots are £57, sir!
£57 !!! But it said £5 in the window!
£5 OFF, sir. They were £62
Crumbs! I-er... I'll have to.. er... withdraw from the purchase ...sorry....
Huh! Tripey shop! Boots will be cheaper out West... all those cows... cheaper leather... ...I'll wait till the first pay day at the ranch... Get the six-shooter dinner time...
GET IN ANE
I wanna buy a Colt 45, bud. Goin' out West!
I'm afraid we haven't a Colt·45 at present, sir. There's a very nice Smith & Wesson·38 I could show you, sir.
Sure. A·38's OK with me, pal.
Here we are, sir, £96
£96! Crumbs! Haven't you got anything a bit cheaper, please?
By the way, sir, you do have a Firearms Certificate?
Er... no... going... ..out west.
U.S.A. sir?
No Texas
Then you will need an Export Licence as well as a Firearms Certificate, also Insurance, and, of course, a Customs Declaration, sir.
Oh, I see well.. I'd be better wait a bit then a firearms... expert... and a customs insurance... I see, sorry... I'd better make further enquiries....
Huh! Tripe! ..be easier to get a gun on The Range ...be lots of second hand... ..I'll wait till I get Out West.... see about the tickets after work..

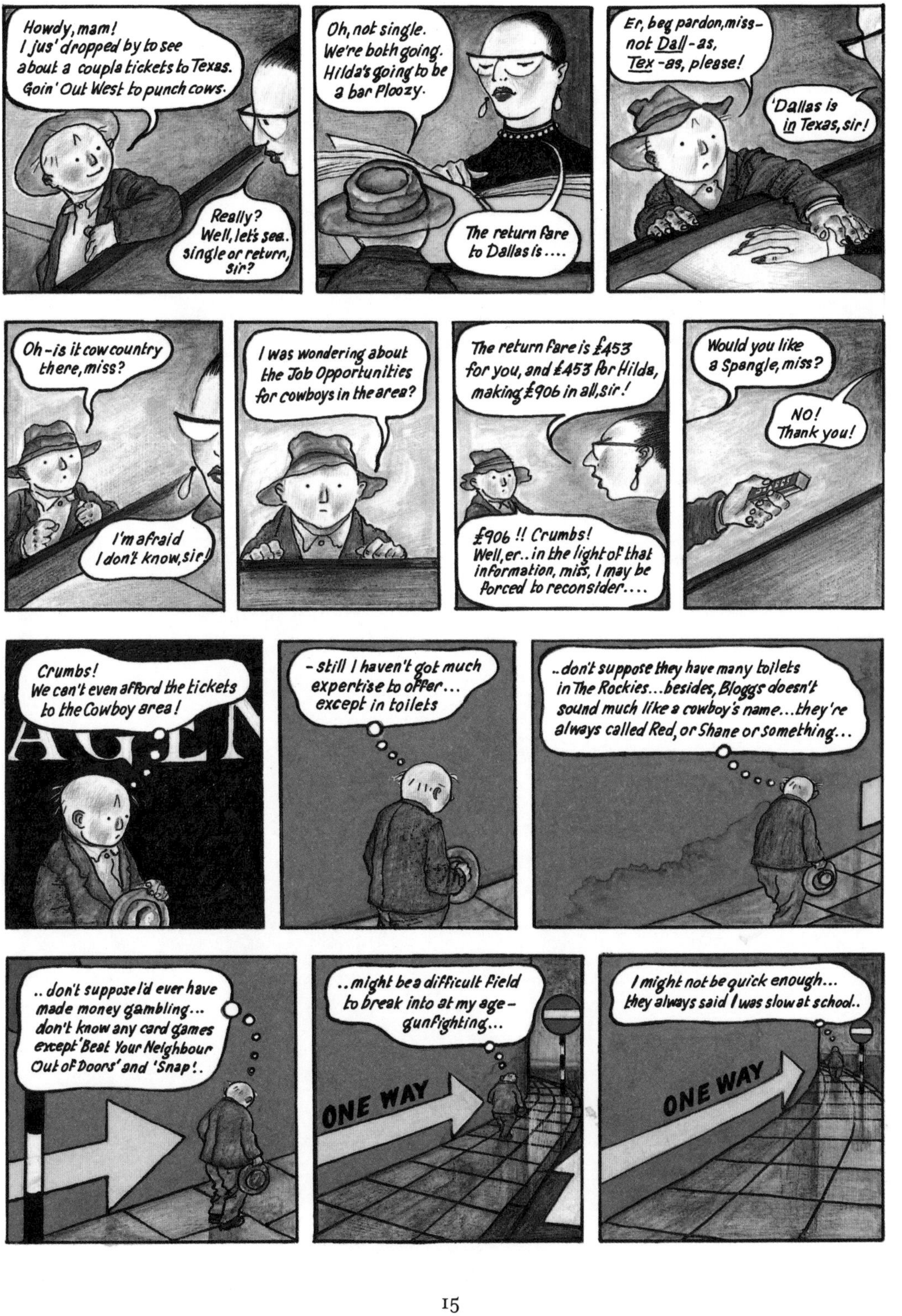

Howdy, mam! I jus' dropped by to see about a coupla tickets to Texas. Goin' Out West to punch cows.
Really? Well, let's see. single or return, sir?
Oh, not single. We're both going. Hilda's going to be a bar Floozy.
The return fare to Dallas is....
Er, beg pardon, miss- not Dall-as, Tex-as, please!
'Dallas is in Texas, sir!
Oh-is it cow country there, miss?
I'm afraid I don't know, sir!
I was wondering about the Job Opportunities for cowboys in the area?
The return fare is £453 for you, and £453 for Hilda, making £906 in all, sir!
£906 !! Crumbs! Well, er.. in the light of that information, miss, I may be forced to reconsider....
Would you like a Spangle, miss?
NO! Thank you!
Crumbs! We can't even afford the tickets to the Cowboy area!
AGEN
- still I haven't got much expertise to offer... except in toilets
..don't suppose they have many toilets in The Rockies...besides, Bloggs doesn't sound much like a cowboy's name...they're always called Red, or Shane or something...
.. don't suppose I'd ever have made money gambling... don't know any card games except 'Beat Your Neighbour Out of Doors' and 'Snap'!.
..might be a difficult field to break into at my age - gunfighting...
ONE WAY
I might not be quick enough... they always said I was slow at school..
ONE WAY

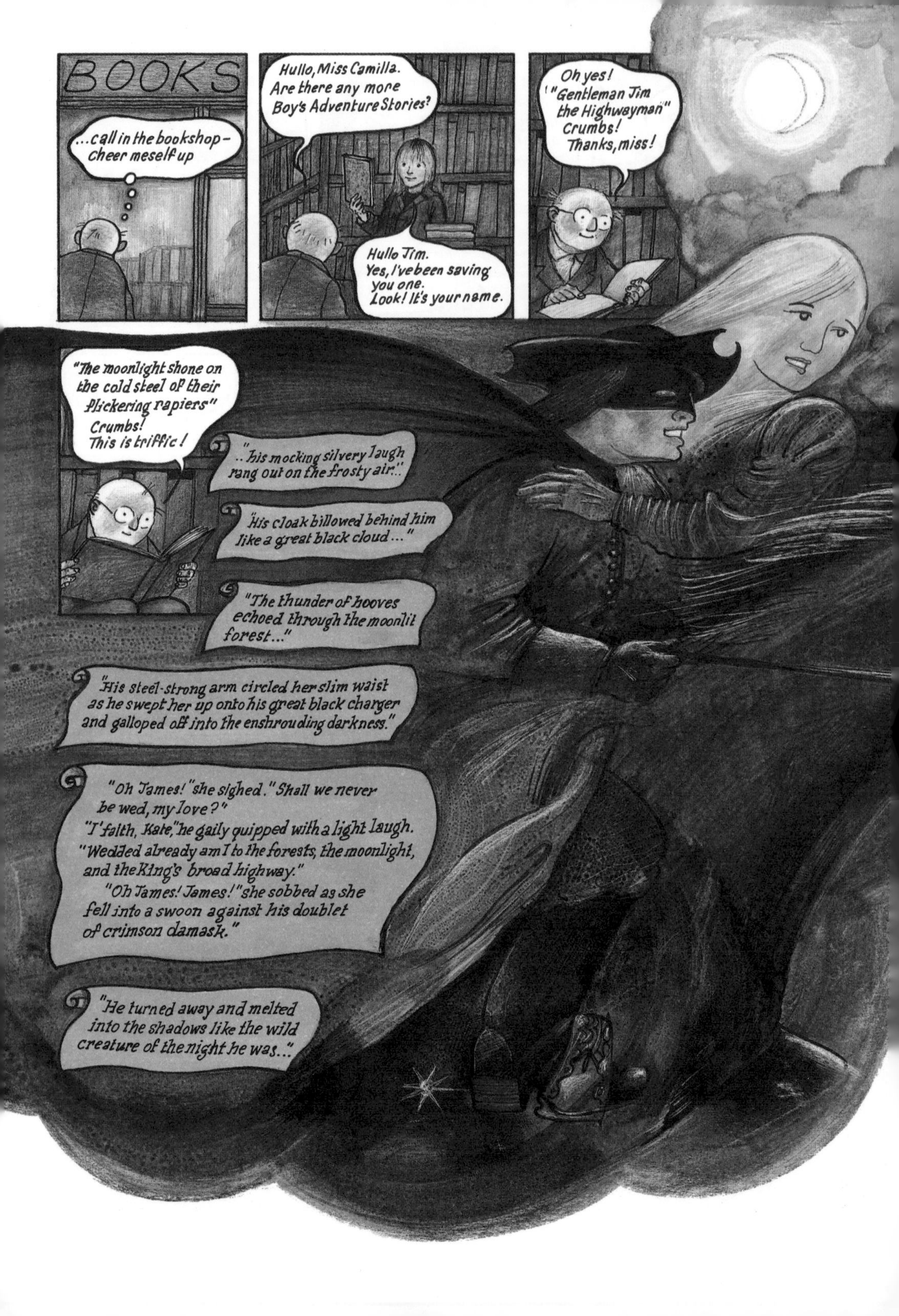
BOOKS
...call in the bookshop - cheer meself up
Hullo, Miss Camilla. Are there any more Boy's Adventure Stories?
Hullo Jim. Yes, I've been saving you one. Look! It's your name.
Oh yes! "Gentleman Jim the Highwayman" Crumbs! Thanks, miss!
"The moonlight shone on the cold steel of their flickering rapiers" Crumbs! This is triffic!
"..his mocking silvery laugh rang out on the frosty air.."
"His cloak billowed behind him like a great black cloud..."
"The thunder of hooves echoed through the moonlit forest..."
"His steel-strong arm circled her slim waist as he swept her up onto his great black charger and galloped off into the enshrouding darkness."
"Oh James!" she sighed. "Shall we never be wed, my love?" "I'faith, Kate," he gaily quipped with a light laugh. "Wedded already am I to the forests, the moonlight, and the King's broad highway." "Oh James! James!" she sobbed as she fell into a swoon against his doublet of crimson damask."
"He turned away and melted into the shadows like the wild creature of the night he was..."

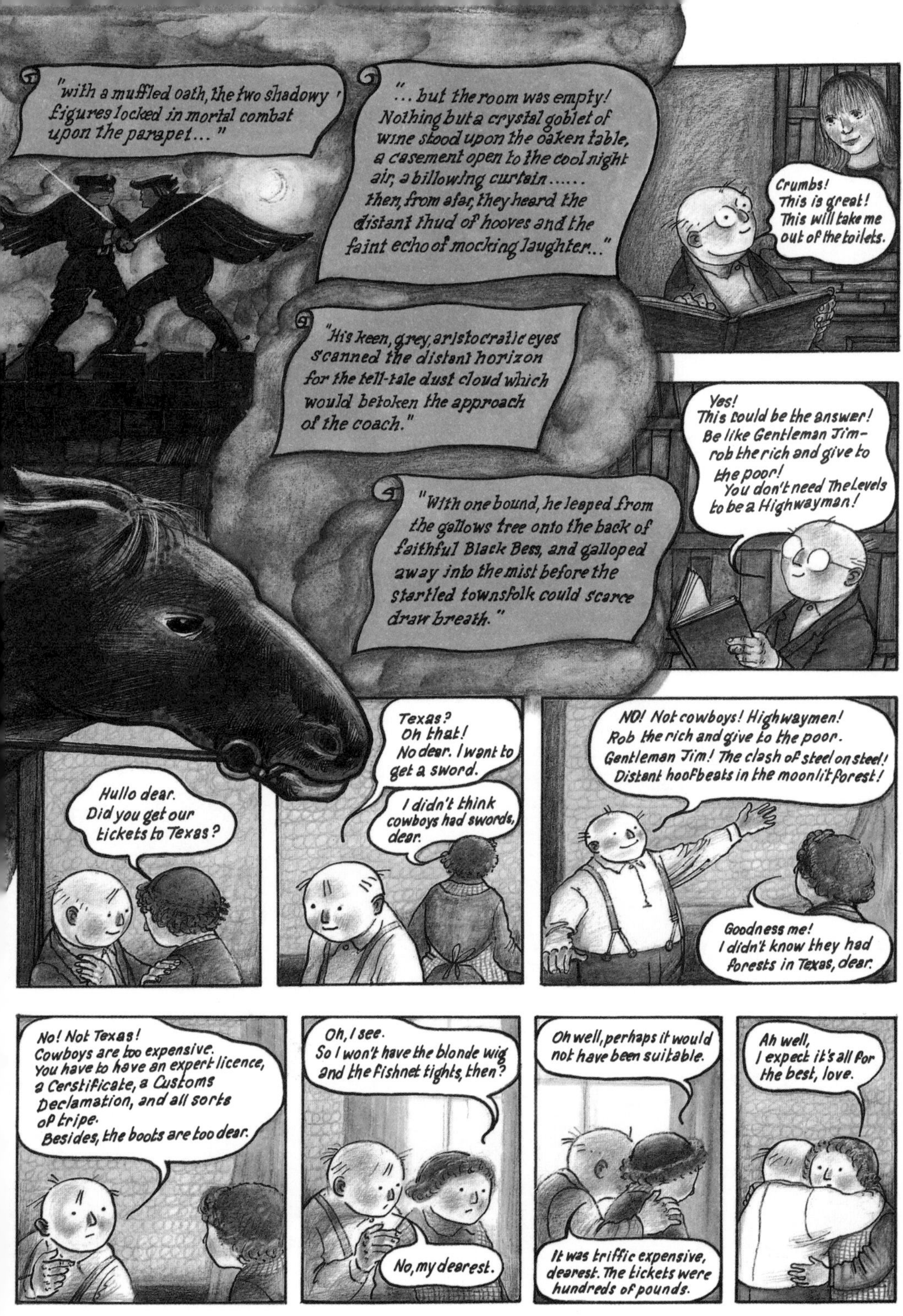
"with a muffled oath, the two shadowy figures locked in mortal combat upon the parapet..."
"... but the room was empty! Nothing but a crystal goblet of wine stood upon the oaken table, a casement open to the cool night air, a billowing curtain...... then, from afar, they heard the distant thud of hooves and the faint echo of mocking laughter.."
Crumbs! This is great! This will take me out of the toilets.
"His keen, grey, aristocratic eyes scanned the distant horizon for the tell-tale dust cloud which would betoken the approach of the coach."
"With one bound, he leaped from the gallows tree onto the back of faithful Black Bess, and galloped away into the mist before the startled townsfolk could scarce draw breath."
Yes! This could be the answer! Be like Gentleman Jim- rob the rich and give to the poor! You don't need The Levels to be a Highwayman!
Hullo dear. Did you get our tickets to Texas?
Texas? Oh that! No dear. I want to get a sword.
I didn't think cowboys had swords, dear.
NO! Not cowboys! Highwaymen! Rob the rich and give to the poor. Gentleman Jim! The clash of steel on steel! Distant hoofbeats in the moonlit forest!
Goodness me! I didn't know they had forests in Texas, dear.
No! Not Texas! Cowboys are too expensive. You have to have an expert licence, a Cerstificate, a Customs Declamation, and all sorts of tripe. Besides, the boots are too dear.
Oh, I see. So I won't have the blonde wig and the fishnet tights, then?
No, my dearest.
Oh well, perhaps it would not have been suitable.
It was triffic expensive, dearest. The tickets were hundreds of pounds.
Ah well, I expect it's all for the best, love.

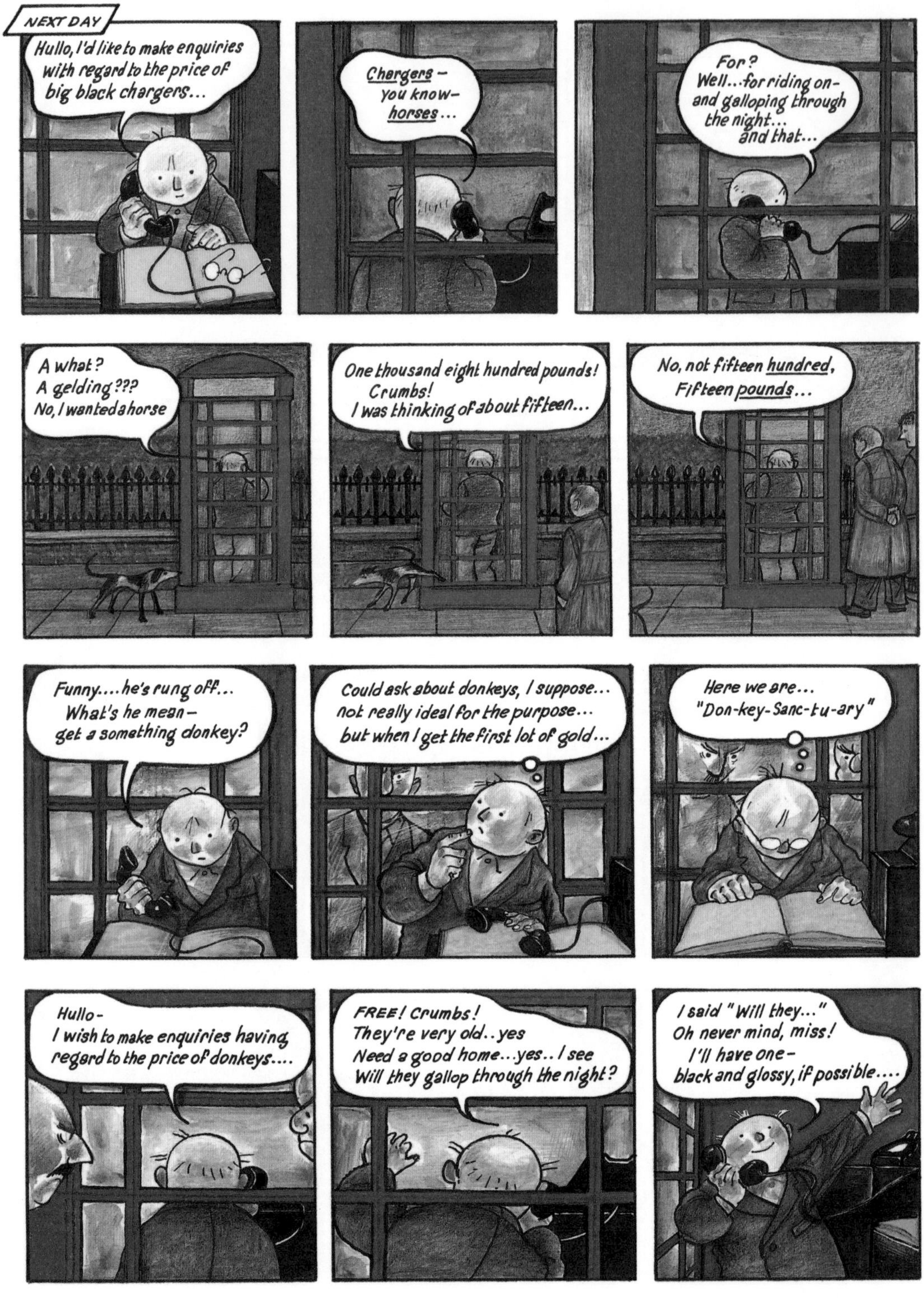
NEXT DAY
Hullo, I'd like to make enquiries with regard to the price of big black chargers...
Chargers – you know – horses...
For? Well...for riding on – and galloping through the night... and that...
A what? A gelding??? No, I wanted a horse
One thousand eight hundred pounds! Crumbs! I was thinking of about fifteen...
No, not fifteen hundred, Fifteen pounds...
Funny....he's rung off... What's he mean – get a something donkey?
Could ask about donkeys, I suppose... not really ideal for the purpose... but when I get the first lot of gold...
Here we are... "Don-key-Sanc-tu-ary"
Hullo – I wish to make enquiries having regard to the price of donkeys....
FREE! Crumbs! They're very old.. yes Need a good home...yes.. I see Will they gallop through the night?
I said "Will they..." Oh never mind, miss! I'll have one – black and glossy, if possible....

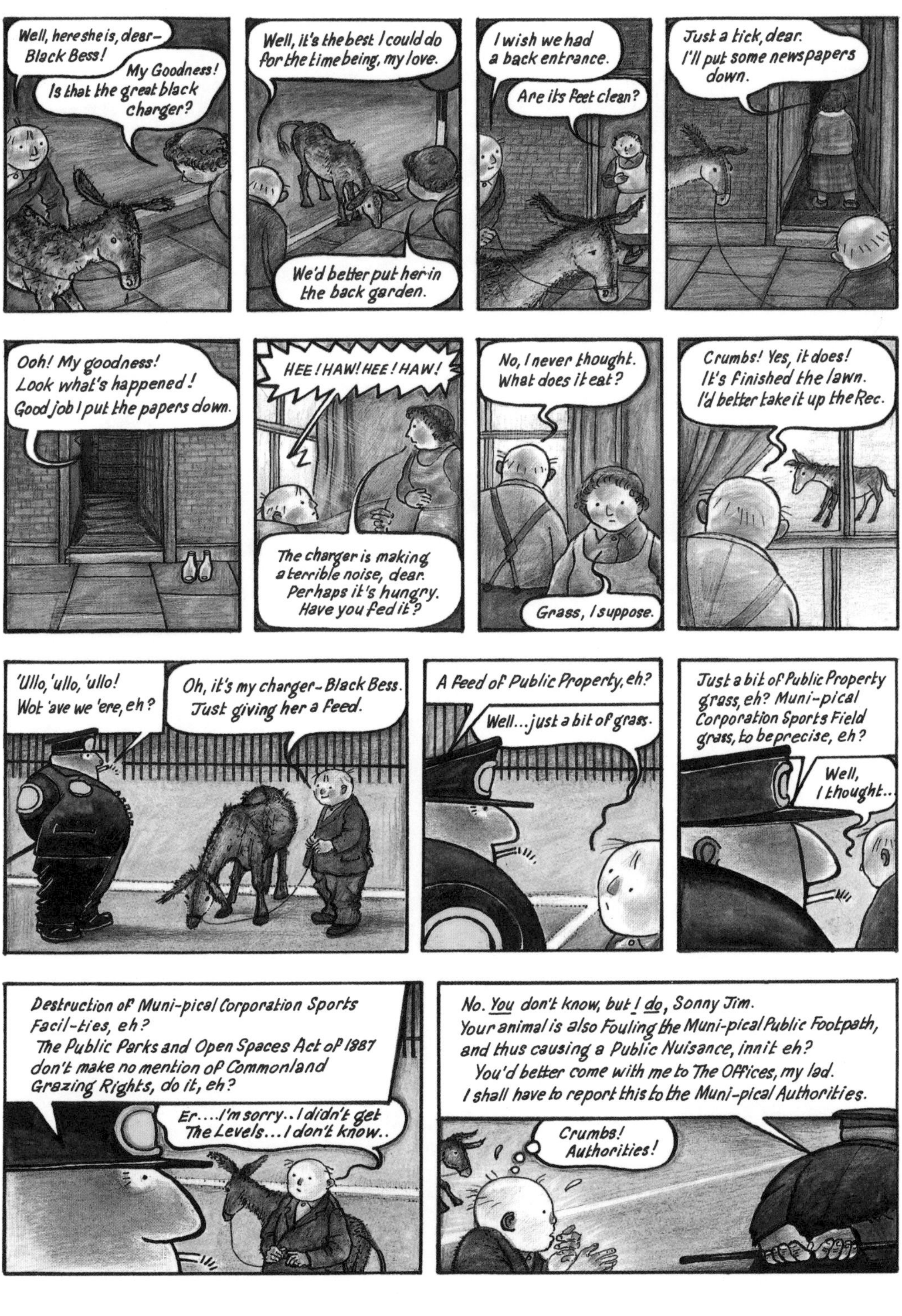
Well, here she is, dear- Black Bess!
My Goodness! Is that the great black charger?
Well, it's the best I could do for the time being, my love.
We'd better put her in the back garden.
I wish we had a back entrance.
Are its feet clean?
Just a tick, dear. I'll put some newspapers down.
Ooh! My goodness! Look what's happened! Good job I put the papers down.
HEE! HAW! HEE! HAW!
The charger is making a terrible noise, dear. Perhaps it's hungry. Have you fed it?
No, I never thought. What does it eat?
Grass, I suppose.
Crumbs! Yes, it does! It's finished the lawn. I'd better take it up the Rec.
'Ullo, 'ullo, 'ullo! Wot 'ave we 'ere, eh?
Oh, it's my charger- Black Bess. Just giving her a feed.
A feed of Public Property, eh?
Well... just a bit of grass.
Just a bit of Public Property grass, eh? Muni-pical Corporation Sports Field grass, to be precise, eh?
Well, I thought...
Destruction of Muni-pical Corporation Sports Facil-ties, eh? The Public Parks and Open Spaces Act of 1887 don't make no mention of Commonland Grazing Rights, do it, eh?
Er.... I'm sorry.. I didn't get The Levels... I don't know..
No. You don't know, but I do, Sonny Jim. Your animal is also Fouling the Muni-pical Public Footpath, and thus causing a Public Nuisance, innit eh? You'd better come with me to The Offices, my lad. I shall have to report this to the Muni-pical Authorities.
Crumbs! Authorities!

23

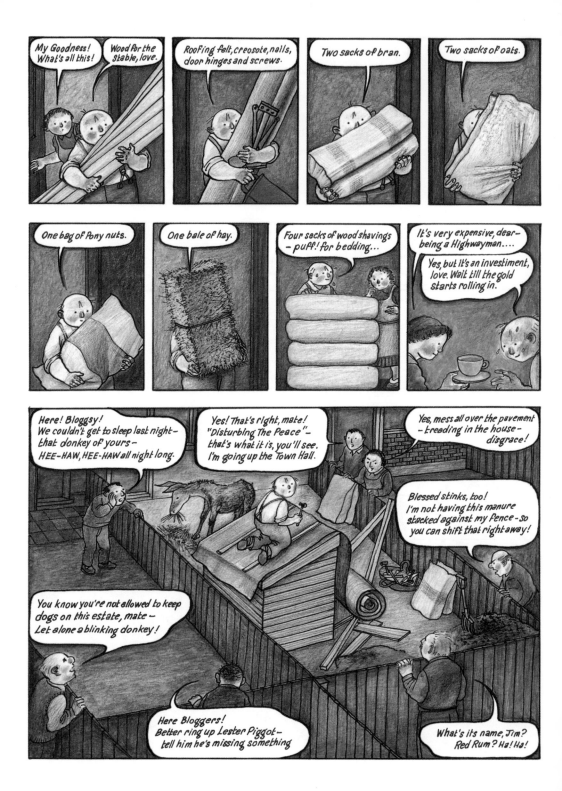

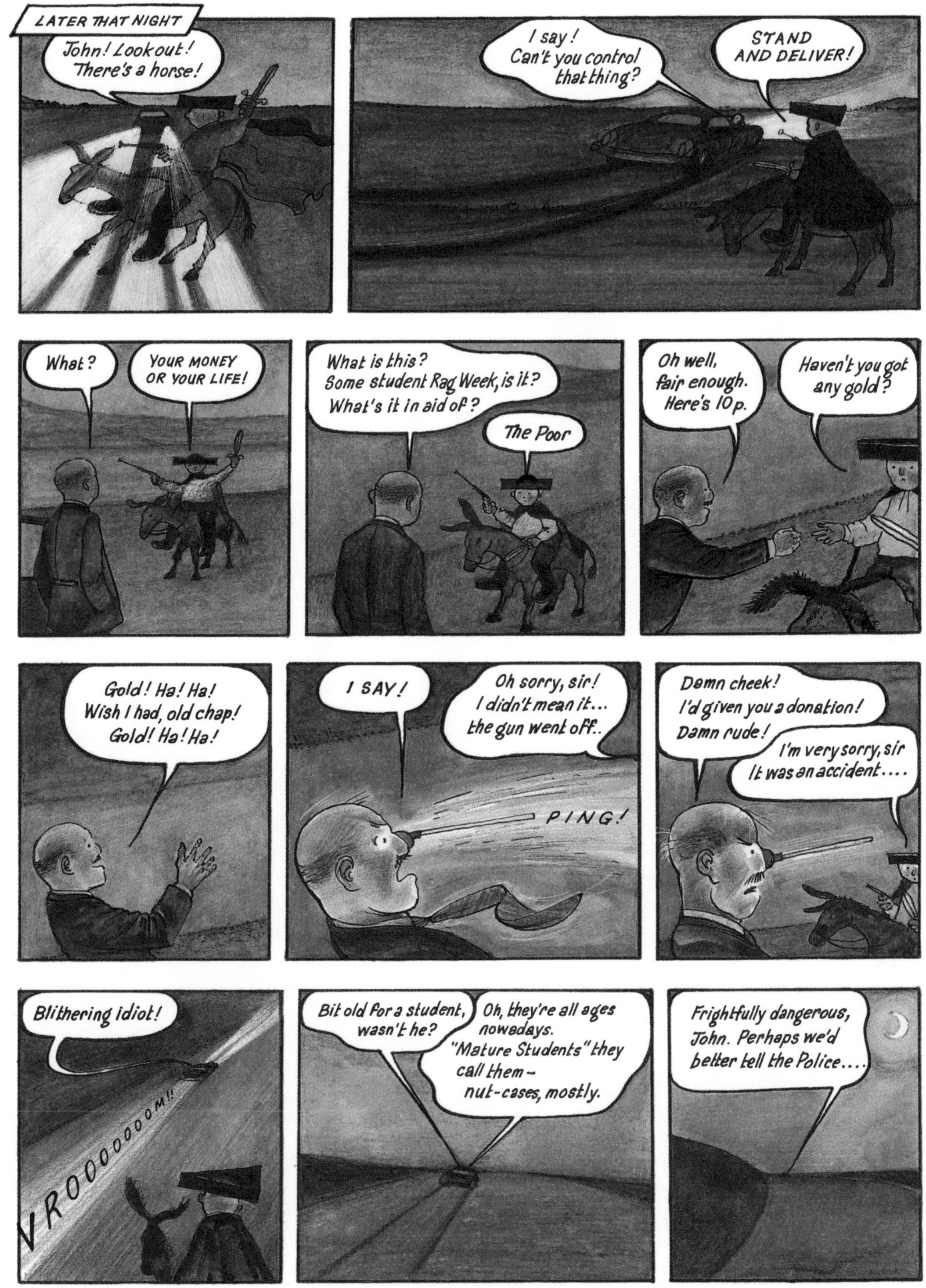
LATER THAT NIGHT
John! Look out! There's a horse!
I say! Can't you control that thing?
STAND AND DELIVER!
What?
YOUR MONEY OR YOUR LIFE!
What is this? Some student Rag Week, is it? What's it in aid of?
The Poor
Oh well, fair enough. Here's 10p.
Haven't you got any gold?
Gold! Ha! Ha! Wish I had, old chap! Gold! Ha! Ha!
I SAY!
Oh sorry, sir! I didn't mean it... the gun went off..
PING!
Damn cheek! I'd given you a donation! Damn rude!
I'm very sorry, sir It was an accident....
Blithering idiot!
VROOOOOOOOM!!
Bit old for a student, wasn't he?
Oh, they're all ages nowadays. "Mature Students" they call them - nut-cases, mostly.
Frightfully dangerous, John. Perhaps we'd better tell the Police....

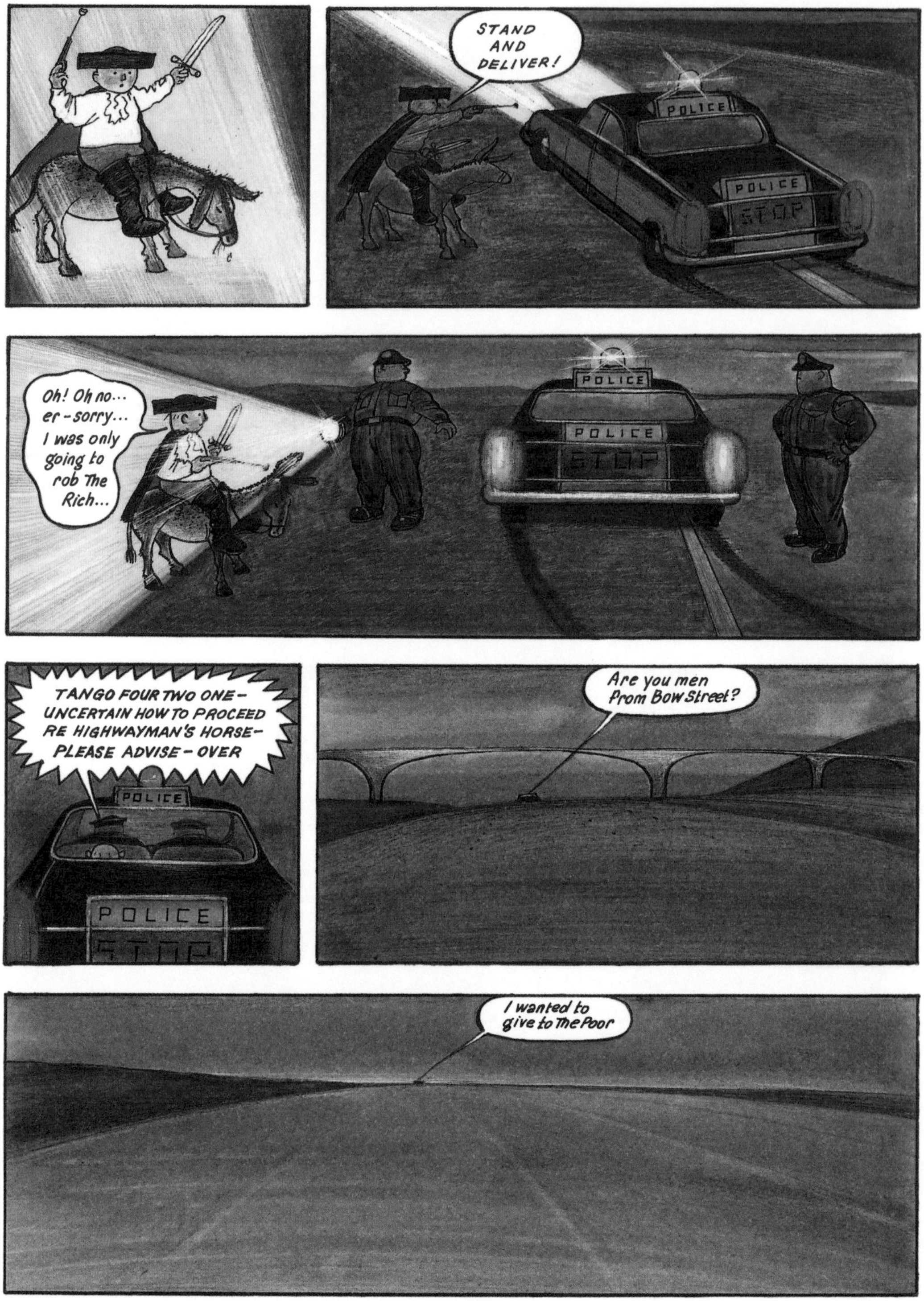
STAND AND DELIVER!
POLICE
POLICE
STOP
Oh! Oh no... er-sorry... I was only going to rob The Rich...
POLICE
POLICE
STOP
TANGO FOUR TWO ONE- UNCERTAIN HOW TO PROCEED RE HIGHWAYMAN'S HORSE- PLEASE ADVISE-OVER
POLICE
POLICE
Are you men from Bow Street?
I wanted to give to The Poor

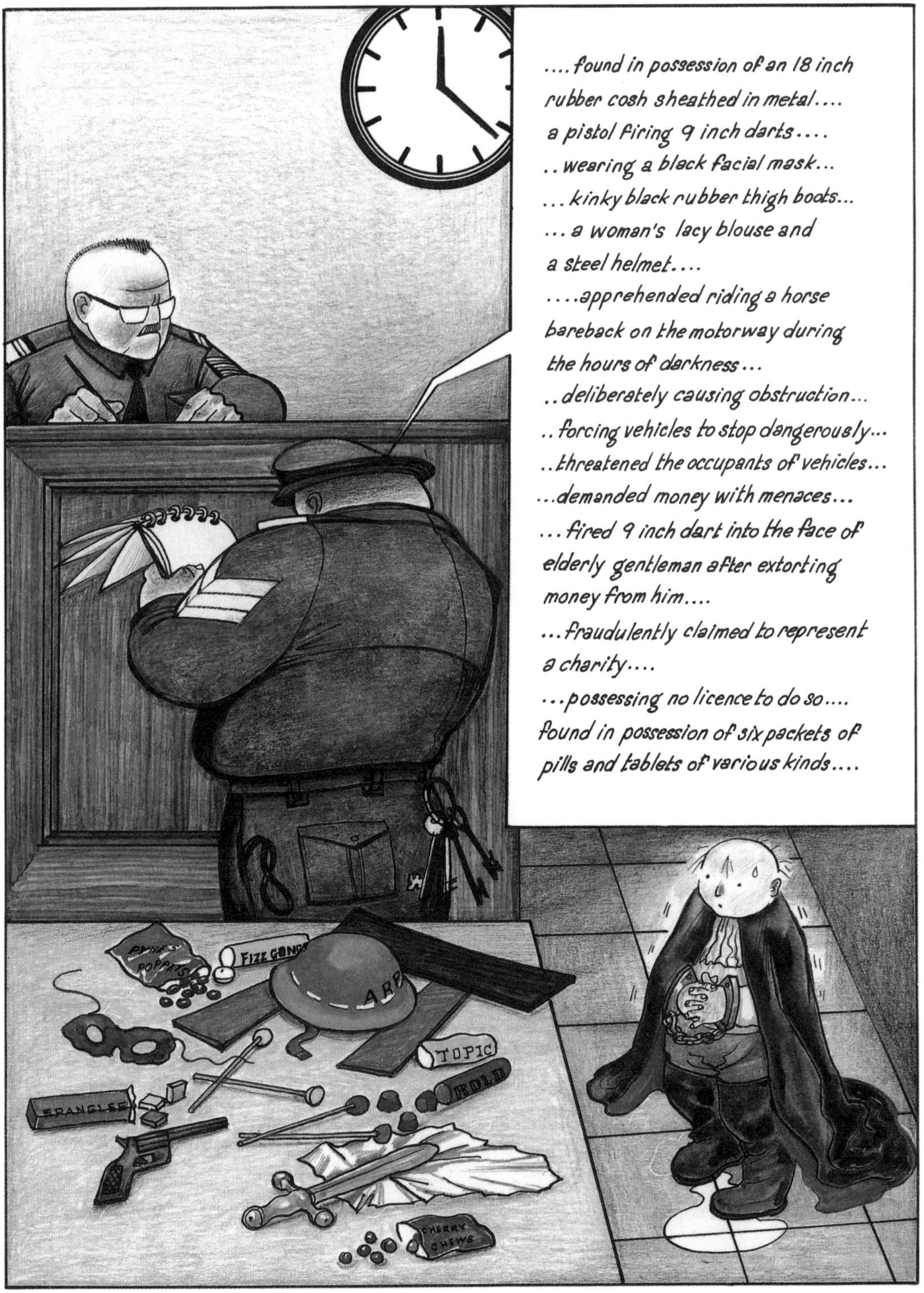

....found in possession of an 18 inch rubber cosh sheathed in metal.... a pistol firing 9 inch darts.... ..wearing a black facial mask... ... kinky black rubber thigh boots... ... a woman's lacy blouse and a steel helmet.... ....apprehended riding a horse bareback on the motorway during the hours of darkness... ..deliberately causing obstruction... ..forcing vehicles to stop dangerously... ..threatened the occupants of vehicles... ...demanded money with menaces... ...fired 9 inch dart into the face of elderly gentleman after extorting money from him.... ...fraudulently claimed to represent a charity.... ...possessing no licence to do so.... found in possession of six packets of pills and tablets of various kinds....
ARP
TOPIC
CHERRY CHEWS

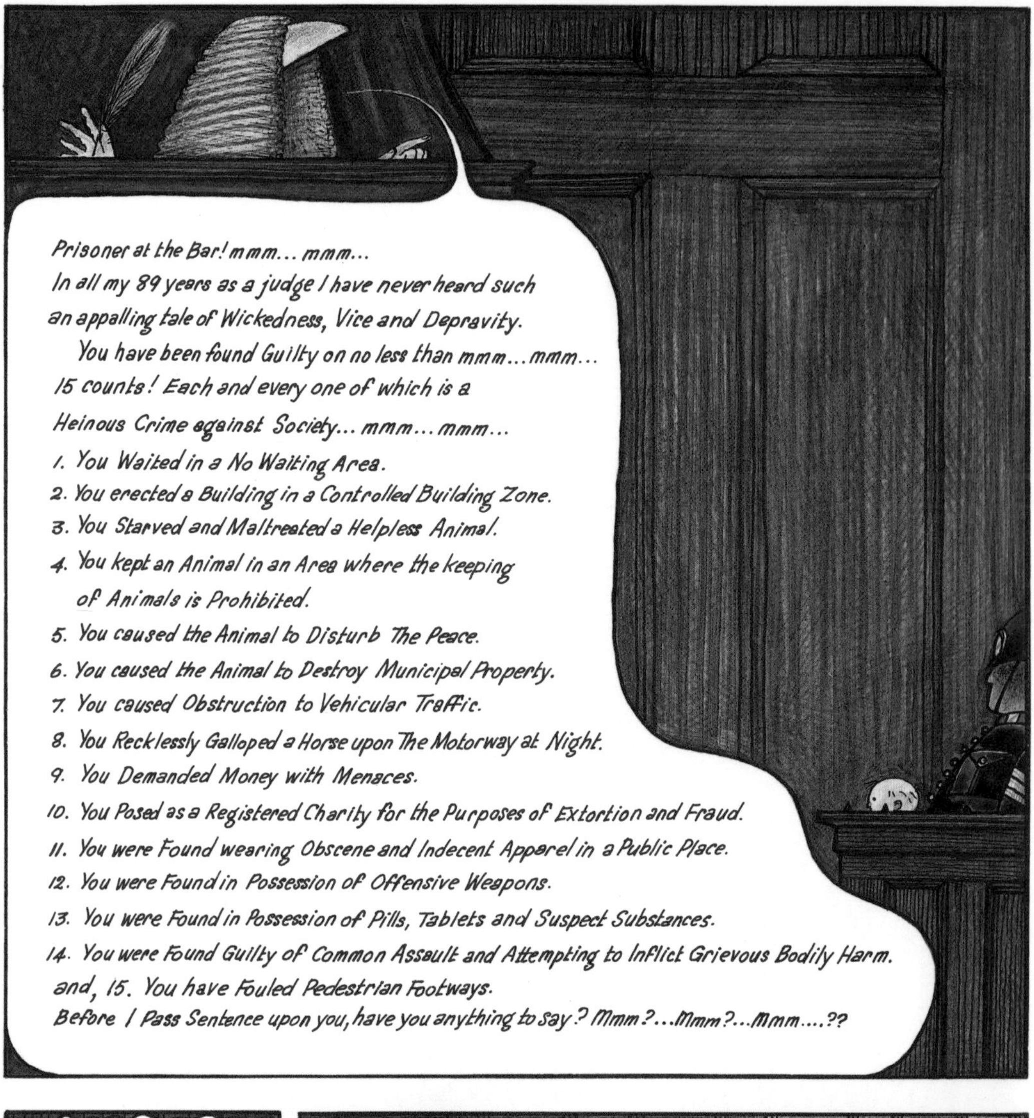
Prisoner at the Bar! mmm... mmm...
In all my 89 years as a judge I have never heard such an appalling tale of Wickedness, Vice and Depravity.
You have been found Guilty on no less than mmm... mmm... 15 counts! Each and every one of which is a Heinous Crime against Society... mmm... mmm...
1. You Waited in a No Waiting Area.
2. You erected a Building in a Controlled Building Zone.
3. You Starved and Maltreated a Helpless Animal.
4. You kept an Animal in an Area where the keeping of Animals is Prohibited.
5. You caused the Animal to Disturb The Peace.
6. You caused the Animal to Destroy Municipal Property.
7. You caused Obstruction to Vehicular Traffic.
8. You Recklessly Galloped a Horse upon The Motorway at Night.
9. You Demanded Money with Menaces.
10. You Posed as a Registered Charity for the Purposes of Extortion and Fraud.
11. You were Found wearing Obscene and Indecent Apparel in a Public Place.
12. You were Found in Possession of Offensive Weapons.
13. You were Found in Possession of Pills, Tablets and Suspect Substances.
14. You were Found Guilty of Common Assault and Attempting to Inflict Grievous Bodily Harm.
and, 15. You have Fouled Pedestrian Footways.
Before I Pass Sentence upon you, have you anything to say? Mmm?... Mmm?... Mmm....??
...er...p.p..please, s...sir I.m..might have b..been..a..b.. better citizen if I'd had The L..L..Levels, sir...
What did you say?
WILL THE PRISONER PLEASE SPEAK UP!
..if I'd h..had L.. L..Levels, your Honours..

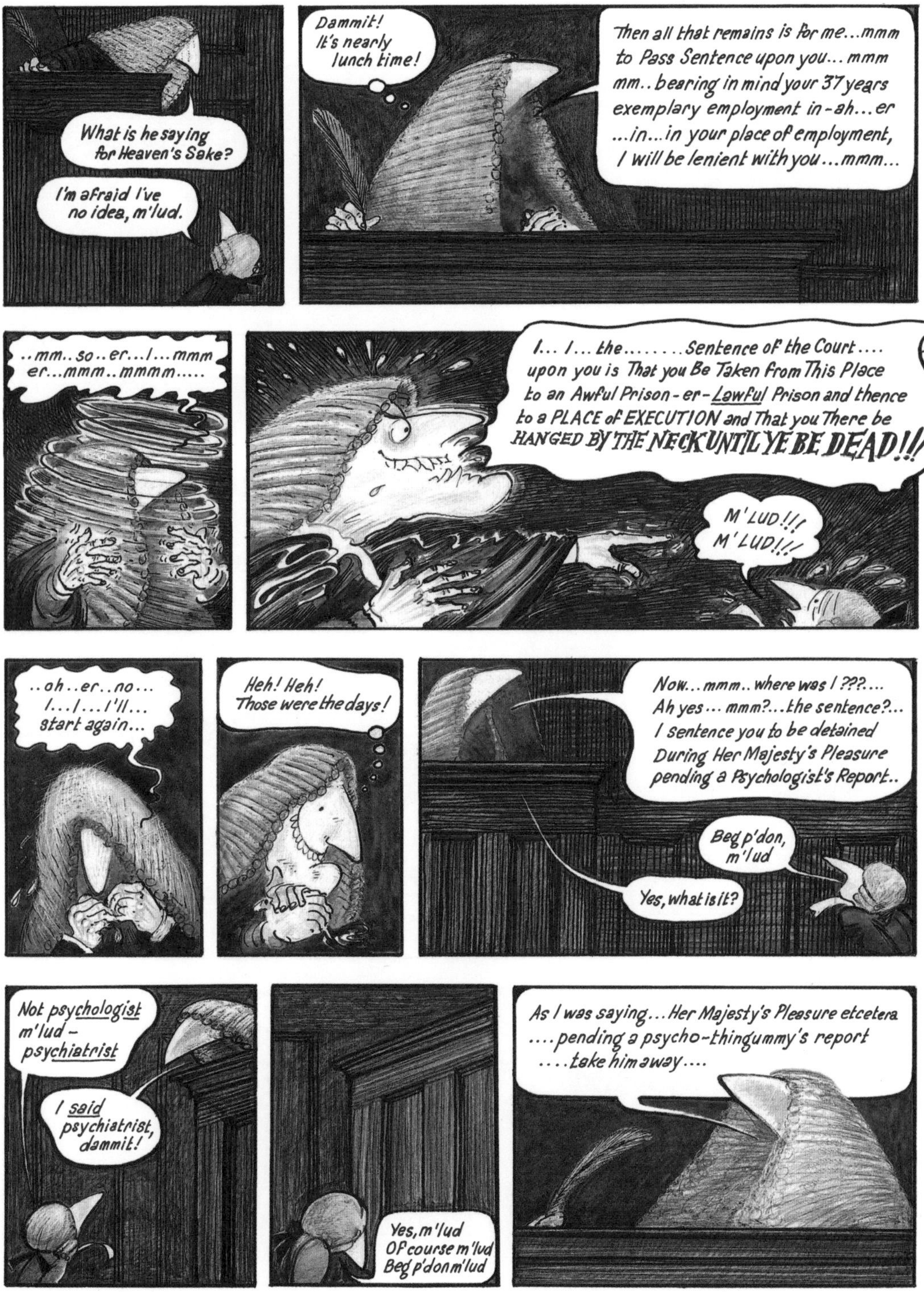
What is he saying for Heaven's Sake?
I'm afraid I've no idea, m'lud.
Dammit! It's nearly lunch time!
Then all that remains is for me...mmm to Pass Sentence upon you... mmm mm.. bearing in mind your 37 years exemplary employment in-ah...er ...in...in your place of employment, I will be lenient with you...mmm...
..mm..so..er...I...mmm er...mmm..mmmm.....
I... I... the........Sentence of the Court.... upon you is That you Be Taken from This Place to an Awful Prison-er-Lawful Prison and thence to a PLACE of EXECUTION and That you There be HANGED BY THE NECK UNTIL YE BE DEAD!!!
M'LUD!!! M'LUD!!!
..oh..er..no... I...I...I'll... start again...
Heh! Heh! Those were the days!
Now...mmm..where was I???... Ah yes... mmm?...the sentence?... I sentence you to be detained During Her Majesty's Pleasure pending a Psychologist's Report..
Beg p'don, m'lud
Yes, what is it?
Not psychologist m'lud - psychiatrist
I said psychiatrist, dammit!
Yes, m'lud Of course m'lud Beg p'don m'lud
As I was saying... Her Majesty's Pleasure etcetera ....pending a psycho-thingummy's report ....take him away....

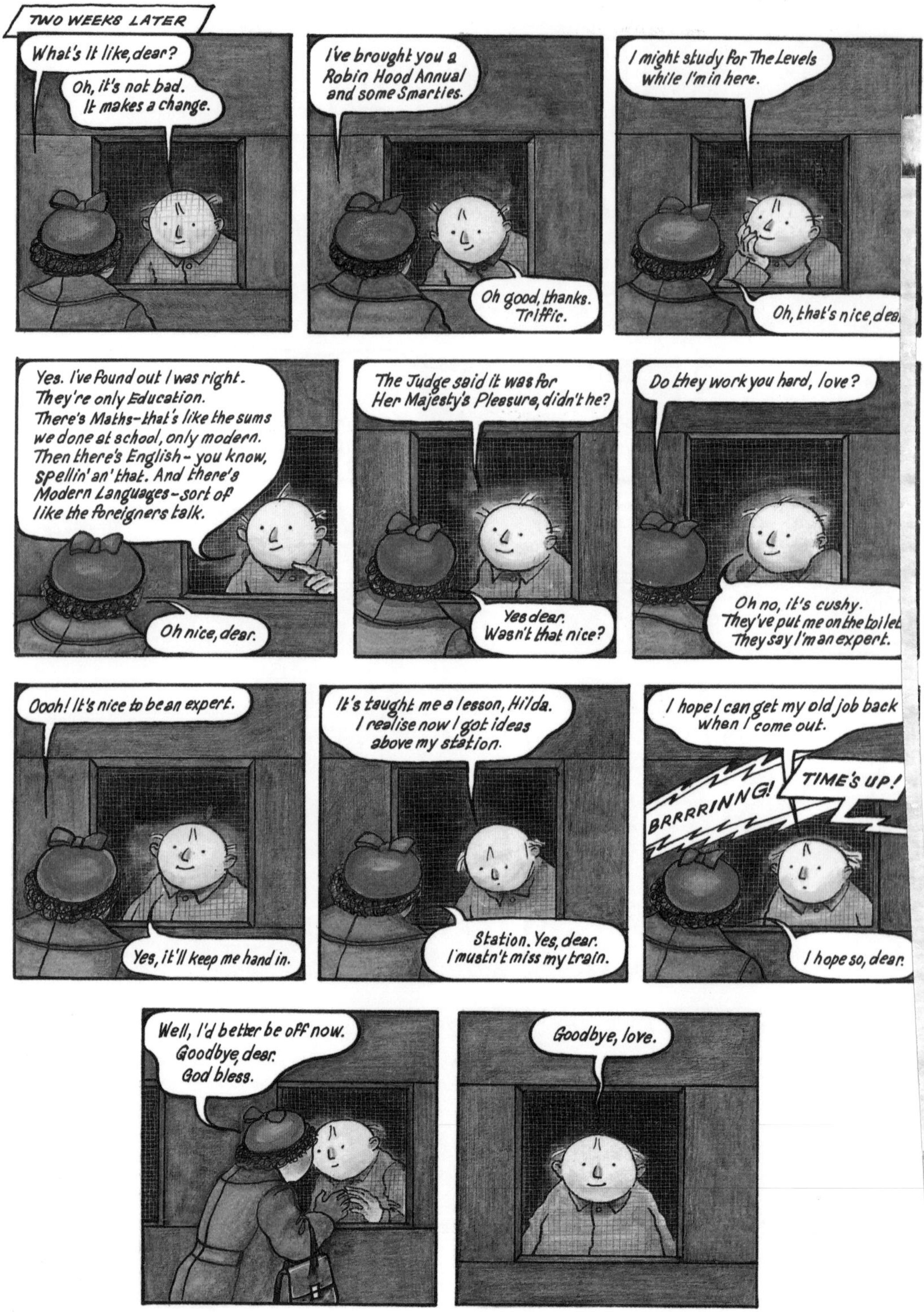

TWO WEEKS LATER
What's it like, dear?
Oh, it's not bad. It makes a change.
I've brought you a Robin Hood Annual and some Smarties.
Oh good, thanks. Triffic.
I might study for The Levels while I'm in here.
Oh, that's nice, dear
Yes. I've found out I was right. They're only Education. There's Maths - that's like the sums we done at school, only modern. Then there's English - you know, spellin' an' that. And there's Modern Languages - sort of like the foreigners talk.
Oh nice, dear.
The Judge said it was for Her Majesty's Pleasure, didn't he?
Yes dear. Wasn't that nice?
Do they work you hard, love?
Oh no, it's cushy. They've put me on the toilet They say I'm an expert.
Oooh! It's nice to be an expert.
Yes, it'll keep me hand in.
It's taught me a lesson, Hilda. I realise now I got ideas above my station.
Station. Yes, dear. I mustn't miss my train.
I hope I can get my old job back when I come out.
BRRRRINNG!
TIME'S UP!
I hope so, dear.
Well, I'd better be off now. Goodbye, dear. God bless.
Goodbye, love.

ABO **OR**

For over 40 years, international best selling cartoonist/illustrator Raymond Briggs has been writing and drawing children's books and graphic novels. Some of his best-loved books include *Father Christmas* and *The Snowman,* both of which have been adapted into films, plays, and animated cartoons throughout the world. Briggs was also an early pioneer of literary graphic novels with *When The Wind Blows,* his brilliant satire on nuclear war. He is also well known in North America for *Ethel & Ernest,* his poignant depiction of the lives of his parents.

Gentleman Jim was originally released in England in 1980 and is now regarded as one of the first English language graphic novels ever published.

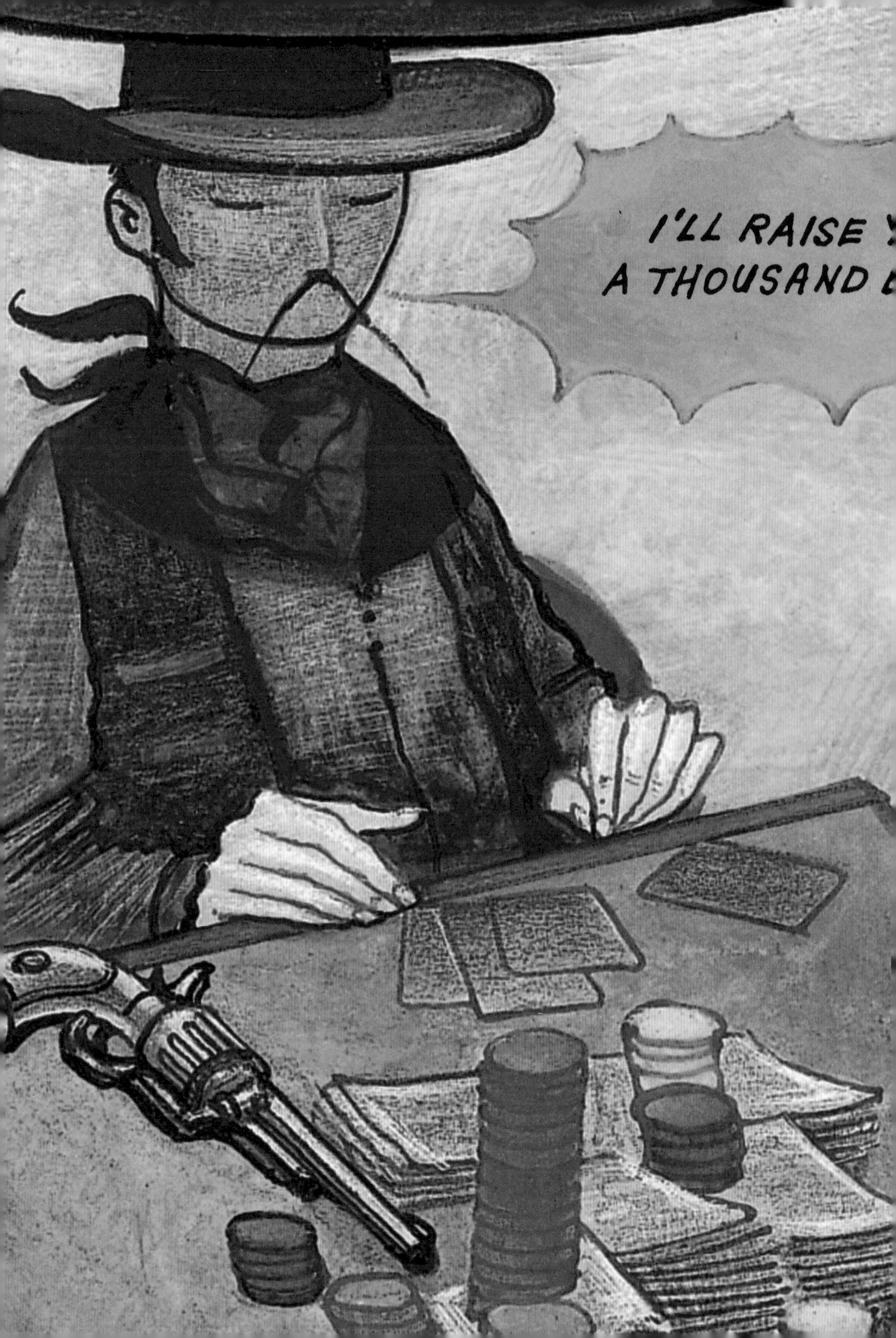
I'LL RAISE
A THOUSAND